Praise for The Pregnant Entrepreneur:

Darla DeMorrow's invaluable  :d
and full of good advice and in d
with running your own busin r
women business owners, whe
already have a baby or toddler.

Martha M. Bullen, Coauthor, *Turn Your Talents into Profits* and *Staying Home*

If you can raise a child you can run a business. But, I know from experience, that doing both at the same time compounds the difficulty of being successful at either. Now, I can only imagine the additional complexity and difficulty added by being the one to carry and birth a child. Frankly, only someone who's been-there, done-that, really understands. That's why I love *The Pregnant Entrepreneur*. It's the first book, I've seen, to uniquely encourage the Pregnant Entrepreneur. I believe this book will give women the confidence and edge they need to create an intensely fulfilling and successful experience parenting while, at the same time, building and running a successful business. Highly recommended.

Michael Port, NY Times Bestselling Author of four books including *Book Yourself Solid*

As all great success begins with a plan, Darla has taken her profession of 'organizing' to a new level! If you desire to follow your passion and blaze a trail for your next generation as you lead by example, this book will not only inspire, but will provide strategies for your success. Children are our most valuable resource.

Cynthia Goch, Author of *MaMa Mia Cucina — A Flavor of Good Food* and *Good Family*

How to Handle
Pregnancy's Physical,
Emotional and
Financial Baby Bumps
– While Running Your
Own Business

The
Pregnant
Entrepreneur

Darla DeMorrow

Blue
Tudor
Books

Published by
Blue Tudor Books
BlueTudorBooks.com

© 2011 Darla DeMorrow

ISBN 978-0-9833723-0-1
Library of Congress Control Number: 2011903953

Cover Design: Deana Riddle

Printed in the United States of America

For Kylie and Lacey
the best assistants ever

The
Pregnant
Entrepreneur

Contents

Chapter 10

Chapter 11

Chapter 12

Appendixes:

Acknowledgements

It takes a village to raise a child, a community to build a business, and many, many friends to publish a book. I don't know how to begin to thank my dear husband, Rich, for all of his support and patience. Although this book is for our girls, it was only possible because he encouraged me in all the right moments, suffered my late nights, and entertained the girls with JJJS and countless other diversions.

It has been said that five years from now we will be the same creatures we were, except for the people we meet and the books we read. Debbie Lillard and Martha Bullen both wrote books that changed my idea of what was possible in my own life. Thank you both for your encouragement and the time you spent with me. Gabrielle Jordan and Maryann Jordan were also a great source of support while this book was coming together. Thanks to my colleagues in NAPO-GPC, who prove that together we are better. Thanks to Pastor Joe DiPaolo, Andrea Hooper, Kelly Raudenbush, and Ali Kresge for your friendship and advice. Thanks to the women who shared their stories and allowed me to include them in the book.

Thanks also to the many clients and business colleagues who worked with me during the early years of HeartWork Organizing. Your smiles, advice, examples, and even hugs confirmed time and time again that women must create more fulfilling lives for ourselves and our families. I am blessed to be working with so many creative and interesting people.

My parents, Gene and Melanie DeMorrow, and mother-in-law Vivian Metzger, also had a hand in getting this book published. Through their transformations from parents to grandparents, I saw that we all continue to learn and grow throughout our lives. Thank you for loving our kids so completely.

Kylie and Lacey, to whom this book is dedicated, I love you. Thank you for making my life more interesting, more lively, and more snuggly. Despite my best efforts, I'm not able to keep you small, so I pray for wonderful, big adventures for both of you. Mommy and Daddy love you—THIS—much.

You: The Business Woman

How to handle pregnancy's physical, emotional, and financial baby bumps—while running your own business.

The absolute best thing about being a woman today is that we have so many opportunities and choices. And all of them are good. Really good. But unlike the women blazing a trail in the 1960s and 1970s, I decided not to buy into the perception that all women must have it all, at least not at the same time. With no plan whether or not to have children, I did what many women do: I delayed having kids until I was almost certain that I would not have them at all. When my happy news came, I was already deep into my identity as a professional woman. In fact, I had already turned a professional corner from employee to business owner. If you, too, are a business owner who is expecting, or an expectant mother who wants to start her own business, read on.

I never planned on being a mommy. Like many women today, I went to school, did the corporate thing, went to school again, and got burned out. In between, I was married, divorced, and finally married to the best man on the planet. After a dozen years in a corporate job, I took a giant leap of faith and left my lucrative profession to pursue…well, I wasn't sure at the time. I ended up starting a great business that I love everyday. Then, I got pregnant.

My first baby, my small business that was not quite three years old, had to grow up fast.

I am not alone. It is estimated that 4.3 million babies were born in the United States in 2007.[1] In 2005 it was reported that twenty percent of American women postpone pregnancy until after their thirty-fifth birthday.[2] The average age at first birth is up more than three years from 1970 to 2000, according to a study from the National Center for Health Statistics.[3]

The term *advanced maternal age* is now commonly used to describe women over thirty-five who are pregnant.

Women who delay having children are more likely to have a college or graduate level education. From 1970 to 2000 the number of women completing college has nearly doubled, and the number of women in the labor force has gone up by almost forty percent. Changes in contraception use, economic cycles, social support, and marriage patterns should also be considered as factors in this trend, according to the same National Center for Health Statistics report.

Women now typically spend ten to twenty years or more in a professional pursuit, honing the skills of their trade, becoming leaders in their field, and earning respect in their communities. Often this time is spent in the corporate arena, where they might spend a dozen or more years working in a pressure-cooker environment.

Women who have this excellent business background might wake up one day and feel the need to translate this education, experience, and drive into a more fulfilling and balanced lifestyle. There are other mountains to conquer, other more fulfilling pursuits. Volunteer and civic commitments beckon as attractive creative and social outlets. Key relationships, especially those with a spouse or partner, may have been neglected over time, and it may require an acute break from a demanding work schedule to bring those relationships back into balance.

The inspired or the downsized among us may leap into buying or creating a small business, perhaps taking a company buyout, a padded savings account, or our partner's steady income to support the early days of the business. This may be a huge challenge especially if most of your reference points have previously been in finding a good job and keeping it. Creating a new enterprise and learning how to run the business end of it is a wonderful and amazing ride.

If, at this point, like me, you decided that you can add a child into the equation, congratulations.

Making Room in My Planner

I always joked that I couldn't have children because there wasn't enough white space left on my DayRunner® to squeeze them in. However, with the deliberate change in circumstances that my husband and I engineered over a period of about six years, I was happy that I could finally make time on my calendar for kids and the care they require. As the owner of my own business, I could set my own hours and make countless other decisions that I could not make as a corporate manager.

The moment I became pregnant, I realized I had made a terrible miscalculation.

Although my husband and I were thrilled to be expecting, I had nothing to guide me during the next nine-plus months. Sure, there were lots of books on pregnancy, health, and learning how to stay home if that's what I chose to do. I had seen numerous corporate colleagues navigate the challenges of maternity leave and re-enter the rat race after a mere six weeks to three months of maternity leave, which seemed like a business eternity. (No one ever took the full twelve months that was allowed per the corporate handbook; that would have been career suicide.) But running a business was a different situation all together. Even though I had professional friends with young families, they all worked in someone else's business. I had no guidebook to help me with the unique challenges of running my sole proprietor business before, during, and after the new addition arrived. Every day I had more questions about how to grow a business and a baby at the same time, but very few people to consult.

Entrepreneurs who want to add a cute little bundle of pink or blue to their portfolio now have someplace to go for a roadmap. This book is for women who already have a business, whether fledgling or well-established, and need to get through the next nine or so months with your mind, your dignity, and your business intact and thriving. Those who aspire to be in business for themselves and are either pregnant or hope to be soon can also learn what they need to know about running a business while pregnant. Starting a business while pregnant is a seriously challenging endeavor, but it can be done. You'll want to pay special attention to the information in Chapter 5 and read Kristy's story in Chapter 6.

There are plenty of other books to help you be smart, sassy, fashionable, and healthy if all you have to focus on is being pregnant. In fact, there may be days during your pregnancy when you think only about your belly, and you are completely defined by your pregnancy. This book will help with the piece of the puzzle that is also deeply you: your business. If you are successful as a small business owner, there is a part of you that is always mentally processing your next business responsibility and action. There is a part that is always calculating your bottom line. And, like me, there might be a part of you that is terrified that your plans for a successful business and a healthy, well-adjusted kid might be incompatible.

Full-Time or Full-Tilt

One of the hardest questions to answer has been, "Do you work full-time?" Of course, it's not at all unusual for women to work outside the home today. Most women today can be grateful that isn't a battle we've had to fight in our lifetimes. Still, the classic mommy dilemma is whether to work or to stay home. Regardless of the pay, returning to a job in someone else's company after only a few short weeks with a tiny new love is difficult. Parenting magazines have articles each and every month about how to stay home or return to the office, but I couldn't do either and be perfectly happy.

Whether to work or not isn't the right question for me and many women today. I want a better life, but I don't define it by more, as in more salary, more stuff, more workplace prestige. I want to have a life where I can be professional, vital, and fulfilled. I want to have my daughter grow up knowing that she can write her own rules, just as I've written my own.

So, when people asked me if I work full-time, I came up with a different answer. I decided that full-time wasn't as important as full-tilt. My typical work day is between two and four hours long. When I'm working, I'm usually super-focused and fully-present. I'm able to schedule things into my day that stay-at-home moms are able to do, like morning play groups, but I'm super vigilant about working during nap time. I've had to pare down my activities, sometimes painfully so, to an honest and realistic workload. After-hours aren't for getting caught up on work like I used to do when I worked for someone else, but rather a time to conduct actual revenue-generating activities.

I'm still sometimes caught off guard when someone asks whether I work part-time or full-time. When someone, even a friend, assumes that my business is a part-time venture because I have kids or because they see me out in the community during daylight hours, my hackles go up. I've learned to simply answer that I own my own business and work flexible hours to accommodate my clients. This usually opens up great conversations to explain what I do and who I do it for, which can lead to some of the best networking and leads. Once people are interested in my skills, I feel less pressured to explain my unusual schedule. Full-tilt seems like a better fit.

Flexibility is good. My schedule is always changing to fit my family's needs. Like a morning person who has figured out how to maximize her peak hours for her most important work, I've defined my life and career in a way that has me feeling good about the time that I spend with family and my business, most days. A lifestyle business lets you define the criteria for spending time on both. You'll write your own criteria for sustainable scheduling.

If this whole run-your-own-business-while-you-are-pregnant thing is sounding like a lot of work right now, let me reassure you that you can have both. Not in the superwoman, militant feminist sort of way that our mothers grew up burning bras for, but in a way that uniquely makes sense for you and your family. Women who are pregnant or have small children are now seen in very public and important positions. You've got to admire Sarah Palin, regardless of her politics, for stepping up as a vice-presidential running mate just months after her son was born. While she was a lightning rod for, well, just about everything, she is one more woman running her young family and a very public enterprise at the same time. You probably have found that the energy you spend on things that are precious to you, as in your family and your creative enterprise, feels completely different than the pressures of working for someone else. You may have already experienced that working harder for yourself is so much more rewarding than working with the hassles and demands of big business, even a big business with good benefits and decent working conditions. So go full-tilt, baby, and enjoy it.

Why You'll Read This Book

Let me say up front, with a dash of reality thrown in, that I am grateful my business existed before I got pregnant. Having some time to focus only on the business is ideal. Building a business is kind of like having a baby, without all the cuddles. If you are already in business, whether large or small, full-time or part-time, the information in this book will help you manage how to transition out of the always-on mode of young entrepreneurship.

This book is especially for women who are running a very small business, maybe even a teeny-tiny business. There are countless consultants, part-time healthcare professionals, landlords, crafters, artists, and sales consultants for Tupperware, Mary Kay, Discovery Toys, Tastefully Simple, and the list goes on, who might not even consider themselves in business. No matter how small, if there are revenues, expenses, and profit or loss, it makes sense to operate as a business. The backbone of our country is small business, and you can be proud that you are part of that. Your business can continue to be small and provide for the needs of your family in important ways we'll cover later in this book. I encourage you to use your small business, even if it is teeny-tiny, to the advantage of your family and your own financial stability. Your business is an amazing asset! You need not apologize for being small. Small, in fact, may be your competitive advantage. This book exists to help you to operate professionally and shrink your pregnancy learning curve.

This book also includes a no-nonsense take on pregnancy topics that you might read about in other books. You are busy, no doubt. You'll get the straight scoop here, with information customized for a mompreneur.

Many women dream of starting a business in order to stay at home with their young children. If this is you, still employed by someone else and looking for a way to create a more balanced life, becoming your own boss may or may not be it. Let's be honest. Small businesses are challenging in every area, from staffing to supplies, finding space to finances, clients to credit. If you do not yet have a business in existence, think about the critical benefits that your employer provides before leaving the confines of your cubicle. Read through this book, run the numbers, and decide whether starting a business while you are pregnant is the right thing for you. If you decide to take on this challenge, good for you. I am rooting for you every step of the way. I know that you can be successful because I have seen it done.

My journey as a business owner-turned mom has proven both more difficult and so much more rewarding than I anticipated. It has taken a few years, but I have a growing service business with a solid client base. I have two young daughters that came along while I was running my business, and I am convinced they are better off being raised by us, and not paid caretakers. I want to encourage you to explore these topics here and find your own answers that will help your family become the family of your dreams. I want to help you not lose your mind as you run your successful business and simultaneously become the mom you want to be.

Critical Questions:

- Do you already have a business?

- If not, what skill or interest can you convert into a business?

- If you are not already pregnant, what is your timeframe for getting pregnant while running your business?

- What is your motivation to become a mompreneur? (Hint: Money is probably not the answer.)

This Is Your Lifestyle Business

What is a lifestyle business? A lifestyle business is a business that you build around you.

Pause on that for just a moment.

Has any place you've ever worked been built around you?

The term *lifestyle business* was made popular with Tim Ferris' book, *The 4-Hour Workweek.*[4] What a great title. Who wouldn't love to have a wonderful, fulfilling and profitable profession in only four hours a week? Sign me up. Despite the bit of hyperbole that comes with the title, there are certain truths that can help the pregnant woman achieve a lifestyle business that is different than the corporate grind.

Technology not only allows us to work from anywhere, it allows us to decide when to work. While some things must be done at certain times (I usually only call clients during daylight hours), other things can be done early, late, or really late, even traditional things like banking. Technology has changed the markets that we can serve, opening up national or international markets for many who would not have previously considered those markets. PayPal and credit arrangements have made purchasing super easy and international currency a non-issue. Technology has also drastically changed our method of marketing. Traditional and expensive modes of marketing have been replaced by inexpensive websites, affordable printing services, and social networks. As Mr. Ferris points out in his book, much of the support you get in a corporate environment, if that's what you are used to, can be obtained through virtual assistants and contract employees that you may never even meet face to face, usually for a very reasonable fee. If ever there was a time to create a lifestyle business, this is it.

How can you take advantage of all of this? The old advice is still true: do what you love and you'll never work a day in your life. Many people dream of replacing their day job with their hobby, even if that means taking a pay cut. While lifestyle businesses can be good sized businesses with staff, hefty revenues, and six-figure salaries for the owner, that isn't the norm. Whether your interests lie in the traditional disciplines or the slightly wacky, the service industry, the manufacturing sector, or the artistic realm, chances are you have some training, talent, hobby or interest you might be able to parlay into a business.

It's the jump from hobby to business that confuses or intimidates some. The U.S. Internal Revenue Service can help you understand the difference. While hobbies may be taxable, they are never tax deductible. Did you know that you can take a loss on a hobby and still be taxed on it? This is not what you want. What you want is a business, even if it is a very small, teeny-tiny business. The IRS says that if you operate your business professionally, as any business would, with the intent of turning a profit, that you can reap the benefits of tax deductions, among other advantages. This is true even if you never actually show a profit. So what is the difference between a hobby and a business?

Not size.
Not hours.
Not staffing.
Not location.
Not revenues.
Not even profits.

What the IRS requires is intent and proof that you are operating as a business. Even though you are having more fun than the average entrepreneur, your lifestyle business should still operate with records, a plan, registration (or whatever is required to legally operate as a business in your state and city) and a separate bank account. With these things (and customers), you can proudly admit to being a business owner.

Do What You Love

My bookkeeper spends about an hour a month handling my account from her home. This is not a big time commitment for her, but she makes good money and doesn't commute, which means she can spend more time with her two small children. Bookkeeping is something she did for years in the corporate world, so she can probably do it with her eyes closed. I'm sure compared to daily kid concerns, this kind of occasional work that she excels at is a fun break from her day. She is using what she knows to create a business she likes doing, but not forty hours a week.

There are many women like my bookkeeper. Fourteen percent of women, in one survey, plan to develop or already had small businesses that they ran during children's naptimes, in the evening and on weekends. Twenty-two percent of all working women worked out of their homes.[5]

Chasing Balance, not Achieving It

A lifestyle business is all about balancing. But if you are looking to achieve balance once and for all, get real. If you think back, you'll probably be hard pressed to find many adult days when you thought life was perfectly in balance. Life is about chasing balance, not achieving it. We practice many disciplines; we rarely master them, because life is always changing. Demands are always shifting. Few things in life are static.

Balance is an elusive quality. We get out of balance when

we have too many outside pressures. Just the thought of having a tiny human being who completely depends on you for everything may throw you off center. The preparation for baby, with the nursery and all the gear, may already be wreaking havoc with your schedule, your sleep, your relationships and your concentration. The other major caretaking activity that can throw a wrench into many well planned lives, of course, is caring for an aging parent. These and countless other outside pressures will demand your attention throughout life. There are also a thousand internal pressures we heap on to ourselves, for accomplishment or self improvement. When tragedy strikes or pressures mount, these strains can seem unbearable. We know that those with strong family and friendship connections are healthier and happier and better able to withstand life's ups and downs. We also know that self-improvement and the efforts to achieve accomplishments are healthy, so why do many of us, especially women, punish ourselves for not accomplishing everything on our list? Just remember, life's pressures are not constant, just as your shape and energy level are not constant during pregnancy.

So let go of the perfect ideal of "finding balance," as if it is something to be earned once in your lifetime and held forevermore. Seek balance in the life you are living right now. One of the best ways I know of to do this is to connect with God regularly. By realizing that He is in control, not me, I gain a little perspective, and this perspective alone can bring me more into balance. Whatever your belief system, this view that there is a larger plan than your own is healthy. Helping someone else also aids perspective in your own life. Formal volunteer programs and random acts of kindness both help you realize that others also struggle to find a workable balance. Knowing we're all going through the same challenges can help you be aware and open to different possibilities for balance in your own life.

During my second pregnancy I had several great opportunities come up, both personally and professionally.

I love to get involved, but I had to gently explain to others and to myself that I could not add more things to my already full schedule and still hope to be a happy person who gets enough sleep. I put several projects on hold for "later." I trimmed my aspirations for a couple of current projects. I added only those projects that helped me in some very tangible, quantifiable way, and I stepped out of some roles entirely. For creative people, there is never a lack of opportunity. Just because we *can* do something doesn't mean that we *should* do it. Seek balance every day, but don't expect to land on it often.

Full-Time or Part-Time Is Just a Box on a Form

A lifestyle business schedule is built around you. I used to chuckle whenever I had to fill out something that asked for my employment status. In fact, it annoyed me that usually the options on the form were either *Full-time* or *Part-time.* How about "full-time, after I finish my other full-time job, which is being mommy?" Or why not call it, "Non-stop, except when I'm sick, and maybe not even then?" I choose not to keep a time card for myself in my business, in part because I always hated them when I worked for someone else. I don't keep track of my hours formally because, well, it really doesn't matter. The fact is that I work the hours I need to work to get things done, and then usually a few more. If you've been on salary working for someone else, you'll realize that you've always been at work the expected forty hours a week, and usually more. In a lifestyle business you have complete responsibility for finding a way to get the work done in the amount of time you allot, or redefine the work to fit the time you want to invest. Either way, you call the shots.

The 4-Hour Workweek assumes that you are able to create a product that you can sell on the internet or through some automated distribution channel, that you can outsource the rest of your daily business to others, and that you can simply inspect and collect your millions during a few hours a week. The rest of your week, Mr. Ferris presumes you will either be climbing mountains or snorkeling in some tropical location. Even if you manage to get the first part of that right, and create a product others find highly valuable, it is still my experience that there is still some amount of work to keep that demand and delivery flowing correctly and continuously. If what you want is a business with enough flexibility to allow you to feel in control of your schedule, and where you can attend to the really important things in your life (which may or may not be snorkeling in the tropics), then the lifestyle business is the ticket.

My own lifestyle business sometimes really is a four-hour workweek. I used to have fun with it and describe my "hooker" schedule by saying I worked nights and weekends in people's homes. I got some raised eyebrows with that description. Now I just say I have a flexible schedule that allows me to work with people when they can meet me. In order to work four hours for which I collect revenue, I am prepping, marketing, training, proposing, researching, drafting, collecting, and administering about four to eight hours. I usually work with clients no more than three days a week because that is all I have childcare coverage. A common rule of thumb in services and consulting work is that you might spend half of your time meeting with clients out of the office, and half or more of your time in the office, even if that office is just a corner of your bedroom. A typical schedule for me looks like this:

> **Monday- Thursday:** play with kids until noon, with lunch by 12:00
> Kids finally down for nap by 1 p.m.
> Conference calls, client calls, and computer work from 1 - 3:30 p.m.
> Snacks from 3:30 - 4 p.m.
> Prep dinner from 4 - 5 p.m.

Play with kids from 4:30 - 5:30 p.m.

Dinner finished by 6:30 p.m.

Baths and bedtime routines finished by 7:30 p.m.

Office work from 8 - 9:30 p.m. or meetings out.

Friday: Work at clients locations while my babysitter watches the kids.

Order dinner out sometime after 4 p.m.

Baths and bedtime routines finished by 7 p.m.

Movie at home with hubby in the evening.

Saturday and Sundays are a mix of me working with clients and my husband spending most of the day with the kids. We usually try to do at least one kid-centered fun activity each day, even if that is just some time at the park.

Daycare Versus Nightmare

Above all, my lifestyle business allows me to decide how my children receive care. Childcare is a very personal decision, often made of necessity, and no one should be judged by the arrangements that they make. I, myself, spent plenty of time in daycare as a youngster. It is unfortunate that Americans have much less choice about their options for early childcare than most other developed countries, where state-sponsored childcare is either subsidized or free. Every day American mothers have to make the decision about whether to work, and if so, where to work, and how to care for their children while they are working. I met a new friend at the playground recently. Her daughter, just four months old, was adorable. When I asked about what she used to do, she got a terrified, frightened look on her face, then admitted that she is a manager for a mega-corporation. She said she'd be going back to work part-time soon, as she protectively hugged her daughter to her chest. Although I'm pretty sure she knew what her body language was saying, she probably didn't know how clearly it was coming across. She was practically screaming that she was desperate to find a way to stay with her baby longer, maybe forever, rather than having to turn her over to a childcare worker and return to a demanding corporate job. This woman has tremendous skills that she could easily transfer into a revenue-generating private consulting arrangement in any number of ways, an option which she is exploring.

Your Lifestyle, as You Know It, Is Over

Your lifestyle business was created because your life as you know it is now over. That's a good thing, by the way. The most repeated phrase a pregnant woman hears is, "Everything changes." That is certainly true. Your lifestyle business gives you the means to do things differently. Isn't that what you wanted? Now you have to ask yourself, if you could do anything you want at this point in your life, as a successful business person with child on the way, what would it be? Now what's stopping you?

Your lifestyle business exists for a reason. What is it? Why are you really doing this? I may have chosen a path with a heavy workload, but I know that most of the choices have been mine, and so I am happy with that path. Knowing there will be plenty of time later for mornings without little people tugging on my pants and asking for Play-Doh® or reading *So Many Bunnies*, I enjoy this version of crazy busy way more than I ever would have enjoyed this same level of busy in a corporate environment. I am proud to pay my own expenses, and I can contribute to my family's financial health. If anything were to happen tomorrow, I could either convert this into a full-time small business with greater income potential, or I could use this experience and all my current connections to step back into a corporate job with benefits. The truth is, I have been hurt before by those I trusted, and I don't want to leave my entire financial well being and sense of self to someone else, even if that is to my husband of fifteen years whom I love so much. I still want to be proud of myself for my professional pursuits, in addition to my current day job.

There is still tremendous pressure from our society, family and friends to do something that matters and hold down a traditional job. Darcie Sanders and Martha Bullen capture this cultural bias in their book, *Staying Home*, noting that, "women in the workforce tend to have skewed ideas of what a mother does all day at home." If your business allows you to physically spend much of your time at home, it may be hard to dispel the notion that you do nothing more than stay at home all day caring for your children. One mother stated, "I no longer qualify as having informed opinions. This can be very stressful for me."[6] Even though it takes work to correct misconceptions about my own business, it is extremely important to my own self-image to stay in the business world and to maintain my own informed opinions.

I want to leave something bigger than myself. I want my girls to grow up in a world where they can really do anything they want, whether the arena is family, home, education, work, or creative pursuits. Other women need not follow my example, but I hope that they will see there is power in being a business owner, no matter what size business it is. I want women not to be afraid of the numbers in their business, or anything else for that matter.

Your Lifestyle, not Freestyle, Business

So you have this business that you've been running for a while, or you are quickly getting up to speed. If you are like most small business owners, you've been running things pretty loosely, and without as much rigor as you might like. People are more successful at anything they attempt if they write down their plans and measure their success. It is likely you have either put off doing a business plan or put off updating an outdated plan because of the work and time involved.

Let's start now by having you take a look at Your Company's Super Simple Business Plan © found in appendix A. This one page form asks you to make clear commitments about what you want from your business and what you are willing to do for your business. With these basic points about your business written down, and your answers to the Critical Questions at the end of each chapter, you'll do more strategic planning in a few hours than the average business owner does in a year. You can use this as a basis for more formal planning, but please start here if you've never created a business plan for your business. Take some time now to flip to the appendix and jot some initial answers to this Super Simple plan.

You want your business to be profitable so you can enjoy your pregnancy and new baby with fewer financial worries. Both businesses and babies are a bit unpredictable. Do your best to plan, building in flexibility for the unexpected. For example, you may plan on working like crazy until your due date, and instead find out that your last month of pregnancy is on bed rest or the baby comes a month early. You may find business activities you enjoy in month four of your pregnancy are things that make you uncomfortable as you near delivery. Or you may find all goes as planned, except that you get an unexpected surge of business, which gives you a bump in revenue, but you need to bring on temporary staff to complete all of your projects and work safely before your delivery. All or none of the above might happen, but it is worth thinking about and planning for various possibilities. If any of these scenarios would devastate your year, then it is a good idea to try to mitigate them now.

By the way, this little financial planning exercise isn't all that different than what your corporate friends are going through. Women on disability for maternity leave do not usually get their full salary, but they may receive either a reduced disability payment or unpaid leave. In either case, their household budgets can be strained. The difference is that you'll be planning your business budget and your household income at the same time. But, hey, you're a professional, a woman, and about to be a mom. You are an expert at this multi-track planning stuff.

Probably the biggest threat to your business revenues and personal income during pregnancy are the physical changes that your body goes through which may cause you to change your work patterns. Many of these are discussed in detail in Chapter 6. However, it bears repeating here that until you experience pregnancy, you won't know what will change in your world. I was completely surprised by exhaustion during the first trimester of both pregnancies. I could barely drag myself through the days. I kept my commitments to scheduled clients, but I really fell behind on the follow up and prospecting that is the bread and butter of my business. As a result, my revenue dwindled severely for a couple of month, and it took a few weeks to build up a full calendar again. The first time this happened, I thought the economy was taking its toll on my business. During my second pregnancy, I knew better, and I was able to plan for this welcomed downtime and relative revenue decline, knowing that I'd have several months of really good health and energy in the second and third trimesters.

If your goal is to lead a more balanced life with time for both family and work, pregnancy may be the best time to adjust your workload so that you can start to settle into a "new normal" where you admit that you just can't do absolutely everything. Remember that four-hour workweek? This is a choice that you engineer. In my case, my pregnancy was the excuse I had been lacking for years to consciously trim my schedule. I started to realize I didn't have to take every job and unrealistically over-deliver on every job if I also wanted a satisfying home life. This made my transition to my time off a bit less abrupt, since I wasn't shifting from 150 mph to 0 mph overnight, but rather making that shift throughout my pregnancy. It also made my re-entry after the baby better since I had already learned that my crazy work schedule really was all my fault, and the corollary was I could have a reasonable work schedule if I decided to create one.

Women, workplace, money, family, success. These are all complex topics, and you're dealing with all of them at once. If you want to make this non-traditional, fulfilling, entrepreneur, and mommy job description work for you, play some possible scenarios through and be open, at least to yourself, about how these changes will make you feel. Even better, discuss these things with your partner and perhaps a close friend who has been objective in the past. Neither your partner nor your friend needs to "fix" things for you, as indeed they probably won't be able to. However, just talking out loud about what is about to happen in your family, business and life will help you be more realistic about these transitions. Talk through the critical questions below with your partner or friends, then complete the Super Simple Appendix A. We'll use it as a basis for more business and financial analysis later.

Critical Questions:

- If you could do anything you wanted at this point in your life, as a successful business person with child on the way, what would it be? Now, what's stopping you?

- Do you have a business plan that supports your lifestyle business?

- Do you have a marketing plan that supports your lifestyle business?

- How will you engineer changes to your current work day to accommodate more flexibility, if that is what you really need?

- What would your daily schedule look like, including time for home maintenance, family and business activities?

- What would happen if you took an extended maternity leave of a year or more?

- What would happen if someone in your family developed a major health issue or got laid off?

- How much of a business revenue reduction (if any) makes sense in the short-term and long-term?

- What if you could only work one day a week?

- What if you can't find affordable childcare when you need it?

A Whole New Field of Study

There is a whole new language that pregnant people use. First there's the big news and the litany of questions that the newly pregnant are likely to endure, such as, "Are you still getting morning sickness?" and, "Do you know the gender yet?" Near-strangers actually get offended if you don't immediately share your due date, because of course, it is extremely important that your baby be born close to their own (or their mother's or their kid's) birthday. Pregnant people can actually visualize calendars in the context of forty weeks. And speaking of math, there's a whole new math to comprehend. In what universe does forty weeks equal nine months? Sounds like ten months to me! Drug companies have even created special little cardboard wheels to help doctors effortlessly calculate this new math; this is not for novices.

There are body parts you never knew you had (or had forgotten since high school health class) that now get names, there are body parts that you only have during pregnancy (like the placenta), and there are moves and maneuvers you never considered that you are about to learn about and practice. (For a quick quiz, flip to the Birth Plan appendix B and see what terms are new to you.) There are special classes to take and birthing trends to read up on. There are cute little names associated with cute little products which will have you exclaiming over and over, "I wish I'd invented that!" And there are things you are about to learn about your anticipated bundle of joy that you may not remember from your bygone days of babysitting. Even more amazing, you'll probably begin to meet this little miracle very soon through the magic of medical imaging.

There are things you'll learn about your partner that you never would have guessed. He'll ask things like, "The baby comes out where?" and, "Do you think he can hear us yet?" You'll also learn how chivalrous your true love really is, how he reacts to the sight of blood, and how excited he really is about another party at your table for two.

In short, this is a whole new field of study.

Malcom Gladwell, in his book, *Outliers*, looks at the way one gets to be an expert. He proposes that one of the critical factors is ten thousand hours of practice, and he illustrates this through examples of the Beatles, Bill Gates, and others.[7] Experts aren't born experts. They learn their skill and practice it to an extreme that most of us never attempt. Since you only have just shy of 7,000 hours to be pregnant, some of which you will hopefully be sleeping, you've got to go another route.

One of the things that creates expertise, or the illusion of it, is the use of jargon. Jargon creates common ground with colleagues in any field.[8] A college professor of mine used to say that if you can learn one hundred key words in any industry, you can fake your way into respected expert status. This is important because, just as you have spent years building an arsenal of professional knowledge, you are entering a world where doctors, marketers, and those who came before you have created a new body of work. Just by reading, you are likely to pick up much of what you'll need to know. It also helps to have colleagues you can rely on for clarification.

The most used phrase isn't jargon at all, but still one you are likely to hear a thousand times just in the first few months after you share your news: *Everything changes*. Boy is this ever true, and in ways you never imagined. Things start to change as soon as you are pregnant, not just after the big day. Are you the Energizer Bunny®, getting projects and proposals out the door without fail? Changing energy levels throughout your pregnancy may force you down for daytime naps for weeks at a time, curtail networking, and require you to modify client activities. Spent years building your own personal style and professional wardrobe? Be ready to pack up most of your favorites for the next year or more, with no good guarantees you'll find suitable and affordable alternatives. Have everything under control? Don't count on it; you'll find yourself apologizing for spontaneous emotions and raging hormones at weird times. Used to giving advice? You'll be receiving more than you thought possible in the next few months, which may irk you or provide a great comfort, depending on your personality.

As much as you need to stay focused on your business and rapidly shrinking window of opportunity to get things done unimpeded, it is a good thing to learn this new language. Being informed about what your body is going through will help you understand what is really going on inside and around you. Right around the Christmas holidays one year, I restarted my lax fitness program on my stationery bike. Within a couple of days, I was experiencing such pain in my knees that I thought I was going to have to get physical therapy. About two weeks later, I found out I was pregnant. What I didn't know was that the chemical called "relaxin," produced by a woman's body to ease the whole expansion process during pregnancy, was already kicking in and throwing off my joint stability. Knowing this, I immediately modified my goals and added ice cream to my regimen. OK, not really, but I gave myself permission to lay off the fitness routine until I got to the next stage of my pregnancy, where I wasn't so wobbly or tired.

Talk about intimidation through jargon, this age of organic, natural, and safety conscious products will have you second guessing everything in your house and on your baby gift registry. It will be almost impossible to learn everything immediately, but there are some great resources out there. Two of my favorites are *Baby Bargains: Secrets to Saving 20% to 50% on Baby Furniture, Equipment, Clothes, Toys, Maternity Wear and Much, Much More!* by Denise Fields and Alan Fields[9] and *Baby 411: Clear Answers & Smart Advice for Your Baby's First Year* by Denise Fields and Ari Brown.[10] Having two books to refer to for a great majority of widely available products and known baby behaviors respectively gave me a little more time to enjoy the baby magazines that cover more of the current trends and hot topics.

How You Learn the Language

In her book called *The Mommy Brain*, Katherine Ellison cited a 1999 study by Helen Christensen which tested fifty-two pregnant women and a control group of thirty-five non-pregnant women on working and verbal memory. Interestingly, she found, "the pregnant women were actually better at learning and remembering words that related to their condition. They perked up, for instance, when they heard the words 'hospital,' 'placenta,' and 'labor.'"[11] So although this is new territory, you are primed to learn about it.

Not everyone likes to read, but almost everyone likes to tell their story. I was amazed at the detail my husband used when telling our birth story after our first daughter arrived. No matter the audience, he shared what I thought were intimate details using very precise language. This is a man who had to be dragged to childbirth classes, but who had assimilated everything as if his next big business deal was going to depend on knowing this stuff. So if you have a friend like this with great storytelling ability, they can be a wealth of knowledge. However, my husband's stories would only be helpful for couples who were planning on having an experience similar to ours. Our experience did not include epidurals, c-sections, or water births. Since every birth story is unique, hearing many different stories is one way to learn the language of pregnancy.

Who Else Speaks This Language

Veterans are all around you. This wasn't completely apparent to me because for more than thirty-five years, I couldn't have cared less about childbirth and its trappings. Sorry Mom, but the best source of information may not be your mom or her contemporaries. Birth trends change, and what was common, acceptable, or even progressive way back when has probably been replaced by something new in the last five years. Hey, even cloth diapers are back in style, but they resemble what your mom or grandmother used about as much as our Bluetooth®-enabled cell phones resemble the Ma Bell Trimline phone. Remember those?

By the time this book is published, there will probably be even better trends and tips to pass along. Just in the last year there has been more of a buzz about organic textiles, BPA-free plastics and bottles, cord blood banking, and new research on autism causes and treatments. The list of new products, trends, and research can and will go on and on and on. Although it would seem that baby store associates might know the most about current gear, this tends to be more the exception than the rule. Depending on whether the store clerk actually has kids, and depending on the size of the store, they might just not be able to keep up with the offerings. Read, read, read, and compare the online reviews for constantly evolving baby gear. Test out the new gear or potential purchases in person if possible. Ask your friends with little ones for their experiences with their gear. They may love a particular item, but use it in a completely different way than you and your partner would. The point is to learn how to make choices for your family, your lifestyle, and your business based on current information along with whatever methods work for your own family.

I have to admit I always equated daycare with nursery school, because in my early years, every kid I knew was in daycare. It turns out that daycare is for those small children whose parents work, while nursery school might be more of an elective option for early childhood education and stimulation. After I became a mom, I learned that playdates are organized get-togethers, which have replaced the spontaneous times when we, as kids, were told to get outside and play with the neighborhood kids. And moms' groups can either be mommy-and-me activity groups where children interact with each other, or moms-only groups where the kids stay home and mom gets some adult time. Either way, moms' groups are a great way to learn from friends who had kids before you did. They've been on the mommy circuit for a while, and they know the lingo. Learn what you can, but keep in mind that there are as many parenting styles as there are freckles on noses.

How to Use the Language With Medical Providers

Bed rest, premature, or c-section are all just words until they apply to you. As soon as you start down this pregnancy journey, learn how to speak to your caregivers about stuff that might affect you, including possible complications. Genetic testing, gestational diabetes, ultrasound, amniocentesis, Group B Strep, the list goes on and on. There's no need to scare yourself, but there is a possibility of unplanned events in your pregnancy. These things might be scary on their own, but they could be devastating to you and your business if you don't have a plan. The good news is that most babies are healthy and are delivered in a relatively routine manner at about the appointed time. But like anything in business, it is good to understand as much as you can so you can make plans and changes as needed.

When the Language Is Not Appropriate

Depending on what you do for a living, your clients, suppliers, and associates might not relate to the challenges that you are going through as a pregnant entrepreneur. There are still, sadly, some professions and groups that might have less sympathy to your changing situation. These folks should not be exposed to your new lexicon unless your business is in the baby industry. Fortunately, blatant discrimination against women doesn't rule the landscape today. However, you can't always take for granted that everyone is treated fairly. If you are in a male-dominated industry or have mostly male clients, be aware that the more pregnant you act and look, the less likely you are to receive the big contracts for the near-term. I'm not condoning this in any way, but it does happen.

For a while you may be able to fly under the radar physically, even if you are already dreaming in pink and blue. No matter, keep professional discussions just that... professional. Two studies from George Mason and Rice Universities point to biases that some people may have against pregnant job applicants. The respondents appeared to be judgmental about the pregnant applicants and held to stereotypes about limited abilities, leading the researchers to recommend emphasizing professionalism, track records, commitment, capability, and confidence.[12] When you do start sharing your happy news, keep the baby talk to benign information like due dates and name choices. Do not share information about doctors appointments, shoe or dress sizes, or for gosh sakes, bodily fluids. The point is, not everybody is learning about pregnancy and babies at the same time you are, and not everyone who has been through it wants to hear how you are going through it, so tailor your conversations accordingly.

Unless your business is mothering and maternity-related products, and even if it is, your professional community does not need all the details of your condition and challenges. Like anything else, there is always the possibility of sharing "TMI," or too much information. This is what I had to caution my husband about after he was blown away by the miracle of birth. I'm blessed that he considered it a miracle, but he did need a bit of censoring for those first few amazing weeks. Except for a few close friends, consider the question, "How are you both doing?" to be the social nicety that, "How are you?" usually is, and answer with a short, "We're great and blessed," rather than a detailed retelling of your own birth story.

Project Planning

By the time you find out you are pregnant, you will likely be two or even three months down the road. That means you are about to have three distinct phases to navigate through in the near future, and we aren't talking about trimesters. It's time to do some project planning.

The first phase of your project is the actual pregnancy phase. There are tons of tasks to care for that you have never considered before. They deal with absolutely every aspect of your life, from A to Z. Literally from the alphabet soup of medical terms to the zippers you can't get fastened, you'll be caught in a whirlwind.

The next phase is the fourth trimester, or the few months immediately after you give birth. This is another great example of jargon you'll never hear until you enter this world of pregnancy. Your friends who work for other people get to go to their human resources (HR) department and negotiate their maternity leave for the fourth trimester. The good news is you don't have to have that HR discussion, and you can take as much time as you want. The bad news is, as an entrepreneur, you probably never really get to "leave" your business. Your maternity leave is undoubtedly going to be interrupted with calls, meetings, and projects.

The third phase in your immediate future will be the settling-in phase, when you actually try to find your new normal as a business owner with kids. You'll find the existing body of knowledge about women in the workplace doesn't completely point to the new normal as an entrepreneur. Almost all of the books and articles that exist for women address either how to run a business or how to be a mom. Not many resources exist to help you do both. But don't worry, this book, along with some soul searching and forward thinking, will help you have a rewarding career in your business while also being a mom, sometimes at the very same instant.

Don't get overwhelmed today. Just get down to the project planning. Focus on the first phase of your project: getting through the pregnancy. Even without formal training, you are probably a decent project planner. With any project, there are three main components. You are charged with delivering your project on time, in budget, and in scope.

Project Baby

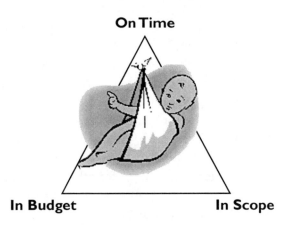

On Time

In Budget   **In Scope**

The on time part has already been defined for you. Your due date is your deadline. You might want to back up your due date deadline a bit, perhaps by a month or more, to allow for pregnancy complications, exhaustion, time to wrap up your big projects at work, or just some quality time before the baby comes. Hey, you're the Big Cheese in your operation, after all, and you can reset the clock if it's the right thing for you.

In budget will probably mean two things for you. You need to consider the business budget and your personal budget. The business budget will require financial analysis, the depth of which will depend on your particular business. If you have partners or external stakeholders with whom you share financial information, you'll need to do more planning than if you are a sole proprietor or LLC who will simply stop operating for a number of weeks or months during or after your pregnancy. Even a sole proprietor will have ongoing business expenses, called fixed expenses, during a period of non-operation. At a minimum, things like credit payments, insurance, or professional dues may continue while you are on your maternity leave. You'll want to do the budgeting (discussed further in Chapter 11) to ensure your business will be solvent when you fully resume your business activities.

Your personal and baby budget may or may not be linked to your business budget. If you draw a salary or if you pay for personal expenses from your business operations, then you'll need to figure in a possible dip in business revenue. If, however, your business only funds itself and certain other discretionary activities (and you don't take a salary), perhaps there will be no impact to your personal budget. This will vary from person to person.

How will you keep this project within scope, and what exactly does that mean? Now is a good time to determine what you want to accomplish during your pregnancy. Something as simple as taking a last couples-only trip with your spouse might be part of your plan. Will you be decorating a nursery or moving to a new house? Do you have a special situation, like having twins or triplets, which just changed your scope? What would you like to accomplish in your business before your due date? Launch a new product or service? Implement new software? Add new staff? These are things that require some planning, and it's best to scope them out and set expectations and deadlines for yourself so you can accomplish them.

An excellent project manager makes use of multiple resources. There are people, processes, and tools available to help get you from here to your delivery. Have you identified your questions and started asking for assistance? Are you going to the right places for help? Your medical caregiver is probably a wealth of information. Are you the type of person who would benefit from a new or experienced moms' group? Groups like La Leche League International (http://www.llli. org) and others usually welcome moms-to-be. Is there a cluster of women who gather professionally in your community? They might be the type of group who welcomes the chance to mentor a newcomer. Websites offered by manufacturers, special interest groups, care providers, and mommy-blogs can also offer plenty of information that you need.

With all of these resources available, be sure to manage information overload. Filter your research to your particular situation, timeframe or interest. Narrowing down the universe of information is a true life skill, and no less so when you are focused on baby preparation.

Outsourcing Your Preparation

As the project manager of this little project, you might feel like you are in a race to the finish. Before your due date, you might want to undertake:

- Home renovations
- Business space renovations
- Product launch
- Networking & establishing key relationships
- Increased media focus
- Travel

Look at a physical calendar and loosely plan out what could take place in the time remaining. Try to plan when you will start to spend less time in the office, if all goes according to schedule. If you are dependant on others (like contractors, vendors, or key employees) to help or deliver something you need, build in a buffer for that handoff. You may find that projects you want to take on just aren't feasible. I started a project to replace our home's windows during the summer. But because of when I started the bids and delays in getting bids back from contractors and long lead times for my chosen products, we ended up with a final proposal that would have had the windows being installed the week before my due date in the fall. The timing was going to be too close. The nursery would have had to be cleaned again because of possible lead contamination during installation, so we decided to hold off on that project. We ended up getting our windows replaced just about a year after I had originally started that project.

Product Management – Baby Edition

Don't you just love new gadgets that make life easier? I may not always be an early adopter of new technology, but when something is really cool or truly makes life easier, I want to shout it from my rooftop. To be honest, when I went to Babies"R"Us the first time, I was terrified. The closest I had been to baby gear prior to that trip was the diaper coupons in the Sunday paper. I didn't have a sister or close friend to go with me, so I was at the mercy of the store clerk and a pre-printed list of must-haves that she handed me when I sheepishly asked if I could create a registry at a mere six months of pregnancy. (Is six months pregnant too soon to be registering? No, it turns out.) While I love boutique stores and service, and you can find absolutely anything on the internet, big box stores are still a very useful place to start. After two hours, my trigger finger was sore from the scanner that I used to zap my chosen items, but I had very little confidence that I had chosen what I needed to keep a small human warm, fed, and happy. (This coming from a woman who moved into her first apartment after the wedding, realizing she had not brought, nor registered for, a set of cooking pans.) Never fear, it is likely that close friends and family at your shower will think of must-haves you hadn't even considered, and if you are lucky, a few gift cards will allow you to fill in around the edges when you bring your little one home. It seems the pilgrimage back to the big box store during the first two or three weeks is a new mom's rite of passage.

Acquisitions:
I Wish I Would Have Thought of That!

As you cruise the aisles and establish your wish list, you'll find yourself amazed time and time again at the cool things you just never knew existed. More than one mom has turned mompreneur or inventor as she created a new product to solve a problem. This might end up being you. An invention can come from a common item that is used in a new way to solve a problem. During both pregnancies, I was always looking for the perfect new necklace, testing my options with a tug. I recently saw a very colorful necklace that is actually made kid-tough from silicone, the same material used in baby teethers. What a brilliant idea. Depending on your business, this time may provide the perfect opportunity for you to branch out into the juvenile market or the convenience market. Keep your options open.

Save your money on stuff you don't need. Although I love cool stuff, the fact remains that I also fight the tide of consumerism daily in order to live a relatively simple life. I love lists (available in the Fields' *Baby Bargains* book, pregnancy magazines and everywhere online) of things you *don't* need. Mommy bloggers are creating new lists every day. Wipes warmer? Plastic disposable everything, including placemats for on the table and placemats for under the table? Matching mobile that can only hang on the crib for six months? Save your money. Stick with the basics, register for a few splurges, and trust that friends will shower you with a few fun picks.

And while we're on the subject, babies appear to be huge

generators of disposable plastic gear on the planet. Think about the length of time your little one will be using some of these items, and think green. Consignment, thrift, online groups, and neighbors offer toys and items that need not be new to be useful. Start building that mommy muscle for "just say no," and quietly return gifts that have the useful life of an English muffin. Hey, I'm not saying deprive your little princess of necessities, but you don't have to start life with 38 stuffed animals, and I don't believe you should ever have to keep duplicates.

Birth Plans and Birthing Options

Since we're talking about planning, it's worth investigating and building in your birthing options up front. Depending on your location, your exposure to this topic, and your peers, you may not realize you even have options. Most women today birth in hospitals, but the options are actually pretty numerous:

- Scheduled c-sections for convenience
- Hospital birth with high medical intervention
- Hospital with choices: midwife, hypnobirth, Bradley, Lamaze, natural
- Stand alone birth centers with midwives attending
- Home birth with midwives attending
- Unassisted home births
- Water births
- Doula-assisted
- Silent birth
- …and more to come, no doubt

A birth plan is more jargon you are likely to hear for the first time when you are pregnant. The birth plan you and your partner will develop allows you to deliberately research options, make key decisions, and maintain some control of the birth event. A good birth plan (or birth preferences sheet, as some like to call it) should also leave flexibility for the unexpected. If you've agreed as a couple on your priorities, you'll be more likely to communicate those priorities to your care providers come crunch time. It's also really good to know that your partner has your desires in writing, since you may not be fully engaged in regular decision making during labor. If he has to take over the decision making for you, you'll both literally be on the same page.

Start with an internet search for "birth plans" or refer to the example in appendix B. This was designed for use in a birth center; since every birth story is unique, you'll revise it for your situation. Share your preferences with your partner and get his agreement to support your choices, or make modifications that are sensible to both of you. There is something very transforming and concrete about putting plans in writing, and this is true of a birth plan as well. Once written, a birth plan helps make the timeline you have remaining very real, and may help you better manage your other responsibilities, knowing that this part of the plan is ready to roll. Try to keep the birth plan a reasonable length, one page or two at the most. Since the birth plan can't cover every situation you might encounter, cover the main priorities. Share your birth plan with your healthcare provider in advance. If there are several different doctors or midwives at your provider's practice, be prepared to discuss birth preferences with each provider you meet. Offer your birth plan respectfully as a thoughtful approach to your own medical care, not as a challenge to your medical provider's experience. Have several copies of your birth plan available at the time of delivery, to allow for staff changes during shift changes, if necessary. Even if things are a little crazy at work just before you head out to have the baby, you'll probably feel better knowing this part of the project has a neat little plan.

Critical Questions

- Do you feel like you can talk to your medical provider and learn what you need to know about pregnancy in general and your situation specifically? If not, do you need to switch providers?

- Who or what is your best resource to learn about pregnancy?

- Does your due date define your stop work date, or would you like to have your business affairs wrapped up earlier?

- Have you talked to your partner about this as a project with three phases: your pregnancy, your maternity leave, and finally settling into the new normal?

- What big projects at work would you would like to complete before temporarily having some downtime in the business (a.k.a. your delivery and recovery)? Launch a new product or service? Implement new software? Add new staff? Is this reasonable?

- Have you looked at your calendar/planner and gotten a visual fix on the time remaining in your pregnancy?

- What are you able to take on before delivery? Will you be decorating a nursery or moving to a completely new house? Do you have a special situation, like planning for twins or triplets, which changes your original scope?

- Have you created a written birth plan that both you and your partner agree with?

- Have you drafted a baby budget? We'll revisit this again in Chapter 8.

CHAPTER 4

No Worries: Identifying and Navigating Through Worries

When fear attacks, take a moment to evaluate what is really going on. Everything changes with kids, and you are in a completely new space here. It isn't unreasonable to be completely freaked out by not being in control for the first time in a long time. Do yourself a favor and recall why you started your business in the first place. Remind yourself that you have been challenged by some pretty amazing circumstances prior to getting here, and you've been able to be successful in ways that many women never have been. You may have to sit down and actually write out an account of some difficult situation you've made it through. By having kids, you are adding a role that women have been succeeding at for centuries. Piece of cake. Let's break it down.

Starting a business is harder than being pregnant and giving birth. A minority of businesses in the United States are started by women. The US government still considers women a protected class and provides advantages to designated women or minority-owned businesses in some sectors. In order to start a business, you must have training or education, capital, competitive advantage, plans, goals, support or mentoring, inventory, staff, and authority to operate as a business. And that's just day one.

Running a business is harder than being pregnant and giving birth. In order to run a business, you must maintain your education or credentials, deal with competitors, forge alliances, satisfy client demands, update business plans, make payroll, execute marketing plans, maintain inventory, pay taxes, network with other professionals, and be the expert in your field.

Getting and being pregnant is probably the easier part of your day.

How will you juggle all the demands of being a business owner as your situation changes over the next months? Everything about being a small business owner is open to interpretation, and that includes how you fold your family into the equation. Bottom line: any answer that is right for you and your family can be the right one.

There are women who barely break stride from the office to the LDRP (translation: hospital labor delivery recovery postpartum room) and back to work again. There are women who take a year out of the professional loop and re-enter only when they have their home life running smoothly. There are women who work only during naptime. And there are a million other variations on this theme. The only situation that isn't legitimate is when you stop allowing yourself to do what you are driven to do. Too many women I meet say they have a small business, but then immediately contradict themselves, and say they aren't really working while the kids are small. *Even a small business can be a legitimate business if it meets the needs of your family and provides financial gain in some form or another.* This is a point that bears repeating, and it should become part of your personal pregnancy jargon.

In order to keep fear at bay, do your research, plan for contingencies, and keep an open mind about how you will structure your work, your family time, and your personal activities.

Case Study:

Robbie is a business owner and financial planner who had a difficult first pregnancy. During her first pregnancy, she almost lost the baby and was forced into bed rest for weeks. She had to rely on her office staff to keep things moving along at work. When her baby was born, she took a chunk of time to be with him at home. While on maternity leave, after researching many childcare options, she placed an ad for in-home childcare. Her list of requirements was long. The caregiver had to be mature, flexible, experienced, dependable, willing to come to her home, and Christian. She was able to find the caregiver that met her requirements, which allowed her to return to working with clients with a reduced schedule for several months, eventually ramping back up to full-time hours. Although her income goals were changed, she continued contributing significantly to her household income while being able to afford private childcare and maintaining a comfortable balance of time with her son and husband. She found that adding a second baby a few years later was much easier since her pregnancy was healthy, she already had a child-care provider in place, and she had a better idea of how to structure her maternity and fourth trimester.

Are you already being kept up at night? From the moment I suspected I was pregnant, I couldn't sleep. At first it was because I was anxious to get confirmation that I was pregnant. Then I was anxious to creatively tell my sweetie the good news. Then I started to mentally redesign and redecorate my house and the baby's room. Then I was worried about the business, and that didn't stop for weeks. "What keeps you up at night?" used to be only an academic question when I was young and slept very well.

It is supremely unfair that sleepless nights sometimes start well before delivery. Unfortunately, they can start even earlier when you have the weight of business planning on your shoulders. You might have a whole carousel of questions interrupting your sleep.

- Can I continue to run the business?
- Will I want to continue the business?
- Will I have enough energy?
- How long will I be sleep deprived?

- Will I have enough emotional support to do both, business and baby?
- Will I like being a mom?
- Will I continue to get new business?
- Will my spouse/partner be supportive?
- Will I still be respected in business?
- Will I be able to make enough money after the baby comes?
- How long can I afford to take off?

These are all the right questions to be asking. The trick is not to drive yourself crazy with these and other concerns in the early, or even the late, stages of your pregnancy. You need all the rest you can get and strategies to help you cope.

If you find your mind racing after the lights go down, try some deep breathing and relaxation tricks. Consciously focus on your breathing, and listen to its pattern. Try to slow down and deepen your breathing. Even if it doesn't clear your mind, it will be good for the health of both you and the baby. If you are a person who races through your day at a breakneck pace, you may be surprised at how deeply and completely a full breath can calm you. After a few deep breaths, continue breathing and begin to focus on different areas of your body where you gather stress, like your face, shoulders, hands, and legs. Working your way from top to bottom, inhale and tense each body area, then slowly relax on an exhale before moving on to the next. By the time you work your way down to your feet, you might find that those carousel questions aren't quite as dizzying as when you started.

One trick I use is running through a mental prayer list instead of a mental to-do list. It helps to take the focus off of myself. There is plenty of time to obsess over all the details in my own life, but obsessing when I am powerless to do anything about the situation is never productive. I usually only make it through a short handful of concerns I have for other people before I zonk out. Mission accomplished.

Give yourself about thirty minutes before you abandon sleep altogether, but don't force yourself through torturous hours of trying to get to sleep. If you can't turn it off, get up and try to do something moderately productive until your body catches up with the clock and begs you for a pillow. If you can, relocate to the guest room or the couch, preferably someplace where you can recline, keep the lights low, and allow yourself to drift off while catching up on your latest trade magazine or business book. Yes, some people find reading stimulating, so try to pick something boring to read, like that insurance policy you've been ignoring for weeks. Watching TV usually won't provide rest or help with whittling down your reading list, so keep the remote control under wraps.

If you find you can't relax in your bedroom, take advice from the experts and spend the next day de-cluttering your room and, if you can negotiate it with your partner, removing the TV from your bedroom. There may literally be too much going on around you for you to find rest, and you desperately need rest, both now and when the baby comes. Don't underestimate the power of a restful room. One note of caution, though, don't try to redecorate in the middle of the night when you can't sleep, especially if you share your space. You'll make much better decisions and get further in the process in the clear light of day.

If you've tried all of the above and still can't sleep, then take action. Keep it low key, but do something besides stewing. All those carousel questions need to be addressed, so find a way to do that. If you are analytical by nature, that's great. Get a pen and start making lists. If you are more creative than analytical by nature, capture your concerns in a way that you can see them; one method for creative types is to record each problem or issue on a post-it note and start covering whatever surface is convenient, like a window or blank wall. Once you see what you are dealing with, you can better categorize, prioritize, and decide how to take action.

There is power in the written word. Once your questions,

concerns and potential crises are written down, you can start to prioritize them and turn them into tasks or projects. Rather than creating a to-do list, which works well for some and not at all for others, just start with a list. Call it a data dump, if that helps. Simply write out, in no particular order, all of those questions that are bugging you. Include baby stuff (When will I have time to set up a baby registry?), personal stuff (Where should I shop for maternity clothes?), and professional stuff (Who will I need to run the store while I'm spending time with my newborn?). Once you have it all down, you can start to break down the bigger questions into smaller tasks.

Just the act of dumping this data onto paper will allow your mind to treat these questions as addressed, even if not answered, and you should start to be more focused. The rest of the questions listed at the end of this chapter should be ones you are starting to noodle through, but they won't necessarily be five minute answers. They may cause you some sleepless nights or long research sessions at your computer. Writing them down and prioritizing them will start to clear your head.

If your business does not yet have a business plan, all of these questions rattling around in your brain are trying to tell you that you need one. Does that scare you? Business plans are long, complicated documents that take ages to draft and even longer to understand, right? Not so. If your business has had to recruit financing, then you probably already have a business plan gathering dust on a shelf. Most small business owners never write down their business plan, and even fewer revise it. The purpose of a business plan is to chart your course and keep you on track when new opportunities or threats arise. Take a few minutes and do a Super Simple Business Plan© on the next page. This is what it says it is…a one-page business plan. Pretty simple. The funny thing is that when you start to fill in the blanks, you'll find either inconsistencies that you need to smooth out, or strengths you can capitalize on. Writing things down, even in a simple format, forces you to organize your thoughts. If you started this in Chapter 2, you might find some of your answers need revising already. If your business has an outdated business plan, you can use this Super Simple Business Plan© to quickly update your status each and every year. Who has huge blocks of time for strategic planning and writing? Not you anymore, mom.

This form with six categories helps you zero in on the major goals for your business. When you answer the critical questions at the end of the chapter, you might find yourself refining some of your answers. Remember that a business plan is never truly done, just like your child is never really all grown up. Go ahead and fill in your answers, knowing you may change the information now or in the future.

Take a moment to fill out the blank form in appendix A. Let your subconscious work on the questions that it raises. We'll revisit it again in Chapter 11, when we'll add even more planning tools to your kit.

Your Company's Super Simple Strategic Business Plan©
(for Year _____)

Revenue	Team
Annual revenue target_____ Annual salary target_____ Retirement funding target_____ Taxable income target_____	(List all the members of your current team below. Also list separately the functions that you need to fill.)
Time	**Priorities**
Target work schedule_____ Number of days per week_____ Number of hours per week_____ Maximum commute distance_____ Training and education targets_____	(List no more than 5 priorities to accomplish or nurture this year.)
Things I Need to Change	**Additional Revenue Streams**
(List items that you would like to make significant changes to in this current year.)	(List any possible revenue streams that you might explore, such as online sales, new vertical markets, or extensions of current business lines.)

Time Off

How much time can you, should you, and will you take off? Like most things in business, plan for the worst and hope for the best. All kinds of variables will enter into your decision of how much time to take off. You may be surprised by how madly you love your little one. Adding some extra time to your scheduled time off to just enjoy getting to know him or her is completely reasonable. It was amazing how much I didn't get done in the first year because I was constantly watching my little girl doing the most amazing things, like sleeping.

It really is true; the time goes by so fast. Your little one will only be young once. Even though I was not then and still am not a baby person, I really enjoyed being around when my daughters were very small. Uninterrupted time is a gift you give yourself, as well as your child.

Some people are terrified of downtime, and I am one of them. If the phones aren't ringing, does that mean the business is suffering? Will my colleagues forget me? Is the dreaded mommy brain a death sentence for my professional life? In reality, I found that the pattern of overwork that has followed me for most of my life continued through my pregnancy and delivery. In fact, despite a very clear intention to stay unplugged for three full months, I agreed to teach a class before that time was up, and I had more than enough revenue-generating work to fill my limited hours when I did begin to schedule my clients again.

Midway through my pregnancies, I started to let my clients know that certain projects they wanted done would have to be scheduled around my three months of leave. By having this conversation in the summer, I had commitments on several solid jobs for the following spring after my maternity leave. While clients don't need to have all the details of your personal life, offering them genuine concern for their needs and being discrete but up front about your constraints will endear you to them. I didn't lose a single client during my pregnancy or maternity leave. In fact, several clients became friends and advocates after seeing my commitment to their projects through a busy and exciting time in my life.

Once you make an emotional decision about how much time you think you might want to take off, go back and be sure to run the number through the worksheets found in the appendixes. You may decide to adjust your planned time off based on your finances. It is always easier to plan for a longer time away and then come back earlier if you decide that is what is good for you, rather than the other way around.

Enjoy Your Days and Friends

Everything changes. Before it does, invest in the important stuff, which probably isn't just your business. One of the reasons you have a business is to be able to lead a more fulfilling and rewarding life. Take time to really maximize your personal sense of who you are, because you will never have quite so much time again. Do what you enjoy. Decorate your home. Spend time in the outdoors. Travel, unencumbered by baby gear and an actual baby. Spend time pampering your sweetheart. Do whatever makes you smile when you think about it. You might not get to do these things again for a while, at least not without paying a babysitter.

Good friends can be easy to find, if you are looking. Just like other transitions in your life, you'll meet new people through your pregnancy and transition into motherhood. There might be other pregnant moms in your neighborhood, or people you meet in birth preparation classes. People come out of the woodwork to pat a pregnant belly, so you might also find yourself drawn to older, motherly types who can be a real source of encouragement and support for you. Old friends can be true blessings, and you might want to invest some extra time in yours these days. Friends who aren't on this same journey with you, especially friends who haven't yet had kids, might suddenly find your interests are so different that it is hard to have a conversation. Or perhaps you had let some friendships falter when your friends had kids, maybe decades ago. There's no better time than now to pencil in time for decaf coffee and some girl talk.

Get crystal clear about what you love in your business. Pregnancy gives you a deadline you probably never would have imposed upon yourself, so use it to your advantage. You will only have another few weeks to complete everything before things change irrevocably. This is almost a version of the old question, "If you only had a month left to live, how would you spend it?" OK, so it's not that dramatic, but still worth asking yourself.

Now is a good time to figure out how to outsource or eliminate all those things you never liked doing. Bookkeeping… outsourced. Web designer…hired. Travel…cut back. Poorly performing products…eliminated.

What do you really love about your business? If it is the people part, whether that is networking, speaking, key client development, or something else, identify it and figure out how to turn that into revenue. Relationships take time to develop, so start right away.

If you love the technical part of the business, but not the sales and administrative aspects, now might be the time to figure out how to become a contractor for some other well-established business. By allowing yourself to spend more time on your craft, you spend more of your day being productive and happy. Other benefits to this approach include increased opportunity for skills improvement and the chance to work more with your colleagues. Best of all, you still get to run your own business as a contractor, although the brand you may be promoting will be someone else's. There are resources for individuals who choose this route, such as www.FreelancersUnion.org, www.Guru.com and www.Elance.com.

Fire your worst clients. That's right. Even at a time when you know your available hours are about to fall off a cliff, and your income is likely to take a dive, dump those clients that drain your energy. Life is too short. When you spend time on projects and with clients who feed your soul, the money is better and your end result is better. Even if the projects they offer are in your target profile, if the client isn't ideal, let them go. If they don't pay bills promptly, are high maintenance, or are a force of negativity, they probably aren't ideal. When I was in the corporate arena, we had certain clients we called screamers; I definitely don't entertain anyone like that in my business today. After my daughter was born, I told my clients that I was no longer actively marketing my business in traditional ways, but I was only working with *fabulous clients*. I smiled every time I said it, and my current clients felt like they were special, since they had made it on to my A-list. There are numerous business experts who will say the same thing, from Michael Gerber (*The E-Myth*) to Michael Port (*Booked Solid*). Michael Port calls it the "red velvet rope policy," as if you are only letting the best people, your ideal clients, inside a red velvet rope to work with you.[13] You can have a multinational business, but the fact still remains that you can't possibly work with everyone, and some clients just cost too much.

Pregnancy Is its Own Time

Nine months can last forever, especially on the front end, when you might be tired, run down, and nauseous most or all of the time. You might be worried you don't have enough time to get through your plan. But things tend to pick up speed, like a snowball rolling downhill, until the due date. Do you remember that when you were a kid, Christmas seemed to take forever to arrive? Now as an adult, Christmas seems to come too quickly. As we get older, we find ourselves saying more and more, "boy, that came quick!" As in, that vacation we planned six months ago, that seemed so far off, is here before we know it. Howard Taylor talks about the concept of internal time, which is the way we perceive the passing of time, versus external time, which is the ticking of the clock. Taylor says our ability to filter out information and events, much like a spam filter on email, affects our perception of time. Life is really measured in memorable events. The more we can remember each meaningful event, the more we recognize the passing of time, and the more we perceive it passing slowly. Routine which homogenizes memories, lack of variety, multi-tasking, and lack of meaningful goals all create an environment where time moves quickly and days pass without much notice. Taylor outlines the ways to purposely slow down time, including having meaningful goals and measuring life by these events, adding variety to your life to make memories unique, eliminating multi-tasking, exercising the body and mind, and getting plenty of sleep.[14]

You would think that being pregnant is enough of a change that the days themselves will be memorable. However, if you spend your days racing toward the finish line (your due date) or somewhat stuck in a fog of nausea and uncertainty about the next chapter, your days will all blend together and be gone in a flash.

Slow things down by being deliberate. Pick a few major life goals and attain them now. Write your book. Visit places you've always wanted to go. Make a scrapbook with your grandmother. Launch a new product you can be proud of at work. Enjoy a season of baseball games with your husband. Decide this is the year you catch each and every local fireworks display. Create a footprint for the next few months that sets it apart from other days in ways that you might never be able to repeat.

Without fail, one of the best ways to accomplish something unusual is to look at your calendar for the next few weeks and months and schedule time for it. Inertia tends to keep us from getting off the mark. If you schedule that Caribbean vacation so far in the distance it seems unlikely it will conflict with anything, you will almost certainly schedule everything else around it. But if you never schedule the cruise at all, you'll be sure to miss it when the ship sails. Baseball games are my downfall. While I love to attend, making last minute arrangements is a hassle. So by scheduling a few games early in the season, my schedule allows us to enjoy the boys of summer. However you do it, make this time memorable, and you are more likely to remember it not just as the short time you spent with a baby registry and a crib assembly manual, but more as a fulfilling and exciting time of your life.

Pregnancy is your new math, and the new math counts in weeks. The construct of forty weeks misleading. At the beginning stages, forty seems like such a big number. Even during the second trimester, you think, "Oh, but I'm not even half way there." But all of a sudden being twenty-six weeks pregnant means you have only fourteen weeks left, and you are definitely on the downhill stretch of your time. Suddenly there are only ten weeks left, and you are huge, uncomfortable, and starting to feel tired again. Oh, and eight weeks really could mean more like six weeks, since a full-term baby can come two weeks before or two weeks after your due date. It sneaks up on you.

Everything happens sooner than you think. For instance, you will probably start to show sooner than you think. Clients will notice, and then you'll have to be ready to discuss your plans, your business continuity, and intimate details like your baby's gender and name. Read the disclosure chapter before you think you need it.

Schedule childbirth classes as soon as possible. Depending on where you plan on delivering, you may need to schedule your childbirth classes sometime during your second trimester. You don't want to leave these until the last minute, in case your baby decides to be the early bird. Like many other healthcare services, childbirth classes are in high demand and do fill up. Especially if you or your partner have demanding work schedules, you'll want to get your best choice of classes on your calendar early. You'll feel more prepared once you learn about your medical care and recovery.

The crib needs to be set up. You need to make arrangements

for childcare. You need to make contingency arrangements for the continuation of your business. You need to make time for your relationship with your partner. All of these things could easily slip during the advancing snowball of pregnancy time, so write down to-do items on your calendar and plan for it all. Not all on the same day, but some forward planning is definitely required.

All of this happens, of course, in the context of your regular work responsibilities, at least for a while. When it comes to work activities, they also can run together and get away from you. Now is a really good time to attend that business conference you might not get to again for a couple of years. Now is a good time to take on a volunteer position you have been considering, so you can learn the ropes before you are sleep deprived. Start a project you've always wanted to take on. Maybe it's not a good time to do all of this at once, but one or more interesting professional pursuits can give you an extra boost on the days when you need a bit more focus or energy.

It Is Over in a Flash

The funny thing about pregnancy is, especially if you have been anticipating this time your whole life, it really is over in a flash. One day you are planning, plotting and running your life and business. The next day you are no longer pregnant, but a cliché of mommy brain and stained shirts. In a matter of hours, the baby lets you know that he or she is arriving, and then you are released from the hospital to return home with less training than you got on how to use your BlackBerry®.

Trust that the baby knows what to do and when. If the process of labor and delivery starts to scare you, remember you are an accomplished woman with many skills, the ability to finish important tasks among them. Remember that women have been successfully birthing perfect babies forever, with modern science and medicine only starting to intervene in the last hundred and fifty years or so. In fact, birthing babies took place in homes prior to Queen Victoria's reign, without the benefit of those great hospital gowns and other modern amenities. Marie Mongan explains how primitive cultures regarded childbirth in her book *HypnoBirthing*. "With no awareness of the link between intercourse and the conception of a child, it was believed that women brought forth children at will. As creators, they were thought to be connected to deity…Birthing was a religious rite, and not at all the painful ordeal it came to be years later."[15] Today you have the benefit of modern medicine, excellent prenatal care, your choice of birthing philosophies, and a myriad of postpartum supports. Whether yours is a long or short labor, it is always relatively short in relation to what comes after. Even if you have an 18-hour labor, remember that this kid is going to be with you for at least the next 18 years, so this is a relative drop in the bucket. Approach this with as much care as you would a product launch or speaking engagement, and you'll be more than well prepared for the few hours you'll spend in labor.

Keep a simple journal. Although I don't usually keep a journal, I do like to keep a brief record of momentous times in my life. Journaling during pregnancy and postpartum can be important in several ways. It can help you slow internal time. It can help document your circumstances, joys, and challenges, which you can share with your son or daughter when they are older. It may help you parse out your own thoughts and feelings in a way you can't accomplish otherwise. It may help you work through some difficult feelings, which is not at all uncommon at this time in your life. About half of all new moms experience some sort of baby blues throughout baby's first year.[16] Keeping a journal doesn't have to be arduous. Appointment books, bullet points and lists, sketches, and saved artifacts can help you shorthand what is going on during your life. Buy a specialized pregnancy journal or a simple spiral bound notebook. Either way, you can begin to create your family's history without derailing your business and professional life.

Start collecting baby and family mementos now. You may be waiting until you can personally stamp tiny feet into the brand-new baby book, but these pregnant days are momentous, too. Record the things that you decide to do to slow down time and enjoy your friends and business during your pregnancy. Save ticket stubs, registry plans, nursery diagrams, travel logs, calendars of your business day, and whatever else seems meaningful in these days. This might also help you get into the swing of saving items that would be great for the baby book later. I loved the format of the baby book I received as a gift for my first child. It provided space in a half page, or essentially a long paragraph, for me to document each month of my child's first year. That seemed very doable, and I was able to capture the important parts of our lives together with about fifteen minutes of writing each month. I added some inexpensive clear page protectors to the book, where I stashed ticket stubs, her first haircut locks, especially memorable greeting cards, and a few other select items. Rather than feeling overwhelmed by a rite of motherhood that often gets neglected, I assembled a cherished keepsake, and it did not take me off task at home and in my business.

Yes, there is plenty you can worry about. But why? Worry is a lack of trust, in yourself, God, and your baby. You take care of yourself and the business. Leave some time for the extra jobs you'll need to tie up and the baby stuff you'll want to enjoy. Spend time with friends you might not hang out with again for a while. Trust that there are higher powers that created this miracle and that will see you through to the end. Document what you can and create action plans for the things that concern you. You can't ask more of yourself than that.

Critical Questions:

- Do you need a pep talk? Write down the three hardest things you've ever had to do or overcome in your life. See? You've already worked on some pretty tough stuff. You can do this.

- What are your options to continue to run the business after the baby arrives?
- What business model will work best for you?
- Do you want to get new business, or simply service your current clients for a period?
- How can you reformat your days now to ensure you have enough energy to complete your work?
- Who will you lean on for emotional support?
- Which friends and colleagues do you want to spend more time with now to strengthen relationships?
- How can you best communicate to your partner when you need support?
- What things can you do to ensure you get enough sleep now?
- What can you do to maintain your professional image throughout and after your pregnancy?
- What kind of income will you need after the baby comes?
- How long can you afford to take off?
- How long do you want to take off?
- What are you doing to slow down time and remember this special time of your life?
- If you're not naturally a planner, what are a few things you really do want to make plans for so you are not caught off guard when the baby arrives?
- Will a journal or scrapbook help you cope or be a burden?

Are You Crazy to Be in Business for Yourself?

There are plenty of reasons to be in business for yourself, and probably more today than ever. If you have a thriving business, you already know this. Many people start their own business seeking autonomy and flexibility. For moms, these things become even more precious. It's a great benefit to be able to do your errands at 10 a.m. on a weekday rather than cramming all of your household responsibilities into a crowded Saturday morning. As a business owner, you structure your day. As a pregnant woman, that's helpful because you can fit prenatal doctor visits and naps in where needed. As a mom, this flexibility becomes worth more than almost any other fringe benefit.

Who doesn't dream of being her own boss? The funny reality is, however, that working for yourself means trading a single boss or chain of command for dozens or possibly hundreds of clients, all making demands of you. You might also be trading the ease of employment for the hassles of employing your own staff.

Being the mistress of your own destiny, however, can't be overrated. When I started my business, one of the things I worried about was that I didn't have a promotion schedule to seek anymore. There was no ladder to climb. I would have to find other ways to reward my own efforts. It didn't take long to realize that my weekly bank deposits were the real measure of my progress, and as they became more regular and robust, I wasn't missing someone else's subjective and sometimes arbitrary evaluation of my abilities. Instead, I had full control over the creativity, lines of business, and execution of business strategy. I could expand into new areas without having to get committee approval and budgeting. I could zig when I saw opportunity, and I could zag when I needed a challenge. I could delight my clients and surprise them with bonus services without seeking approval. My business evolved three times in one year to ensure that I could offer a full menu of services to my target market.

One of the best reasons to be in business is unlimited income potential. Sure, you may have a set pricing menu and only so many hours in the day, but there are ways you can extend your business beyond just your abilities, whether by hiring staff, outsourcing some of your business, or adding products and services to your base. No one will dictate that you can only earn a three percent raise each year, or that you've hit a salary ceiling based on your pay grade, as is often the case in the corporate environment. Alternatively, you may find ways to improve productivity to keep the same income but reduce the number of hours you work. Any mom would choose to work less and make the same, or possibly more, through the efforts of their business versus a corporate job. Studies routinely show this to be the case. Over thirty percent of respondents in a Salary.com survey state that they would prefer time off over a $5,000 increase.[17] These numbers are repeated in surveys nearly every year. If you are able to make that switch and buy back some of your time, consider yourself lucky. Many of your corporate colleagues aren't so well off.

The tax benefits of owning a business are a secret that is well known to savvy entrepreneurs. It has been said that there are two tax systems in this country; one system is for employees and one system is for business owners. Every small business owner that applies this automatically gives themselves a raise, since a dollar not spent on taxes is a dollar that you earn and keep. By claiming every legal tax deduction, audit-proofing your records, and taking advantage of government programs that apply to small businesses, you can seriously impact your own financials for the better. There are plenty of activities, such as the use of your car, entertainment expenses, and use of your home for a professional office, that a business owner can legally use to offset or reduce income. Corporate employees do not get these tax breaks. I'll repeat myself for emphasis: a dollar of taxes not paid is as good as a dollar earned. For this reason it is critical that small business owners get good, substantiated advice from tax experts, such as knowledgeable CPAs and accountants or resources like the Small Business Administration (www.SBA.gov) or The Bradford Tax Institute (www.bradfordtaxinstitute.com).

Business owners are in business to make money; there is no escaping this. There is also no denying that owning a successful small business, no matter how small, has emotional benefits as well. Career downtime doesn't have to exist for small business owners, because your career can develop alongside your family's growth. You can maintain your professional identity, which you may have spent years cultivating. Or you have the chance to develop an alternate professional identity that is closer to your dreams. Just as important, you are positively modeling an example for your younger family members. You demonstrate that they have options as women, mothers and professionals. If this is important to you, there is no better way to teach achievement and potential than showing how it is done.

What Type of Business

Do what you love and the money will follow. Well, it may not be that simple, but if you spend your days doing something you hate, you are not likely to be successful in all the ways you want to be. If you spend your time on a craft or service that you love, at least that part of the business will bring you pleasure, your customers will see that, and you'll generate more energy to take on the next business challenge.

If you find you are a person who loves *doing* the business, but you find you don't like *running* the business, that doesn't mean you are destined to be an employee. You might still decide to be in business for yourself, but act as an expert independent contractor providing services for another business owner. This can, in some cases, still provide you all the financial, tax, emotional, and flexibility benefits that you might otherwise get as a sole proprietor servicing your own clients.

Entrepreneurship allows you to leverage your past experience, even if you don't want to do the same job. Many entrepreneurs translate their past experiences into completely new ventures. Peers from my high-tech days took their business acumen and started businesses such as pet spas, tax preparation services, or design firms. You need not be limited to the job function you held in a previous life, but you can cross disciplines and trades to build something entirely new. More than one accounting manager has left behind a cubicle for the chance at artistic fame and fortune. But your corporate skills may bolster your small business. A sales job in your past gives you a tremendous set of skills to network and build relationships as you position your own services in the marketplace. Any business owner who thinks they aren't in sales is fooling themselves, but you don't have to be slick to sell yourself. Simply telling your story and positioning your services as something that will solve problems for your clients can make you wildly successful. In fact, the more authentic you are, the more likely you are to develop genuine relationships that can lead to more sales, more profitable sales, and customers who refer you to other potential customers.

Case Study

Andrea is the mother of two small children and a proud former member of the Air Force. She and her husband met and married while both were stationed at an Air Force base. Shortly before she became pregnant with their third child, she founded a business that funds a non-profit foundation that produces film documentaries about military history. The foundation provided a critical link for Andrea to do something that she loved and felt strongly about. It was also the perfect way for her to build her civilian resume and job skills. With her young family, it offered the flexibility she needed to run errands, meet family commitments, and still exercise the part of her brain that thinks in military terms. Her business is based out of her home, and will travel with them when she and her family make their next move with the military.

Today you can be in a traditional or completely virtual company, or some combination of both. If you provide services, such as copywriting, bookkeeping, or other technology driven services, you might be able to run your entire business through the postal service and from your spare bedroom. Bring on the bunny slippers! However, even in a virtual business, there may still be a fair amount of face-to-face networking and business development that you need to do outside of your home office. In a more traditional business, you might be required to visit clients or operate a store front or office where the public visits you. If your current business operations don't suit you, when you become pregnant is the time to make the change.

Creativity on a Rampage

Some women worry about the dreaded mommy brain and the inevitability that their life will unravel due to lost brain cells. Very early in my pregnancy, I began to feel less capable and more forgetful. I was very relieved when I learned what was going on, thanks to a book by Katherine Ellison called *The Mommy Brain*. The research on mommy brain shows that women are more focused on different things during pregnancy than they were before they were pregnant. Not fewer things. Not simpler things. Just different things. Craig Kinsley, a neuroscientist at the University of Richmond, Virginia, compares the pregnant brain to a revving race car in his article in *Scientific American*. Neurons ramp-up activity and grow during pregnancy, getting ready to focus on the newborn and decipher needs and wants despite the newborn's lack of language. Neurons in the hippocampus are posing to enhance concentration and memory, all needed to track a newborn's activity and focus in on things that are important to the newest family member.[18] Ellison's book references this same Mr. Kinsley who characterizes this time as a "reorganization," or a "tradeoff for a better functioning and focused brain later on."[19] *The Mommy Brain* presents researcher after researcher who explains this forgetful, uncertain time as an evolutionary explicable outcome. Our brains aren't operating poorly, just on a different level. Ellison quotes Allan Snyder, an Australian neuroscientist, who says, "Einstein was known to forget where he put checks of large amounts not because he had a bad memory, but rather because of his deep concentration on things of greater importance."[20] You might not be accused of being an Einstein at this point, but it helps to know that you are in distinguished company. So give yourself credit for keeping track of all of your current creative and business pursuits while adding a whole new dimension of caretaking, all while your brain is going through a major reorganization. An occasional mommy brain moment is bound to happen, but you are still probably performing better than you think you are, on the whole.

Apparently, the brain actually rewires itself during pregnancy to hyper-focus on things required to protect our young. Have you ever noticed how many great new children's products are created by new moms to solve problems they were having? If you haven't yet, you will. There are an estimated five million mompreneurs. In fact, moms start new businesses at twice the rate of any other segment of the population. Mothers represent a $1.7 trillion buying market, so it makes sense to build for and from them.[21] One great example was featured in the following clip.

Mom's Invention Cleans The Grime Out Of Sippy Cup Straws

March 25, 2010 by Angela Shupe

As any parent knows, a sippy cup that was lost and suddenly materializes a few days later isn't a pretty sight. Depending on what was in the cup it is almost guaranteed that the liquid has congealed or simply clogged up the built in straw, rendering the cup useless. Of course that would mean you'd have to make another run to the store and buy yet more sippy cups, a task that is just as costly as it is frustrating.

Jennifer Reyes was frustrated too. She was tired of trying to clean out clogged and unsanitary sippy straws. No matter what she tried to use, it just didn't seem to work. At that moment a lightbulb went off in her head. Putting her frustrations to work, Jennifer created the Sippy Straw Cleaner.

Tell us a little about the Sippy Straw Cleaner and what inspired it.

Have you ever accidentally left your child's sippy cup in the blistering hot car or wonder what that odd smell is coming from under the couch, only to find your child has hidden their thermos there over a week ago? Have you ever gone to pick up your children from daycare only to see some other runny nosed child drinking out of your child's sippy cup? I am a stay at home mom that has tackled the never ending battle of trying to disinfect and clean out the curdled milk or molded apple juice from my children's sippy cup and thermos straws. I tried using toothpicks, pipe cleaners, Q-tips, even small paintbrushes... always with minimal success. I never felt confident that it was bacteria free and clean enough to have my children drink through it again. After throwing away TONS of expensive sippy cups because of dirty, clogged straws, I came up with the idea for a mini reusable straw brush cleaner... and voila ... the idea for the Sippy Straw Cleaner was born.

Besides sippy cup straws, what are some other uses for it?

We've had lots of fun feedback regarding what people use the Sippy Straw Cleaner for. Let me list a few:

- Drinking straws
- Sports bottle straws
- Medicine Droppers

63

- Jewelry
- Parts of a "keg"erator
- Grooves of sliding shower door track
- Hummingbird feeders
- Scratching the insides of a cast on an arm

What was the idea to launch process like for you?

A bit overwhelming!! Being a stay at home mom of two kids, going to school full time for a second degree, launching Sippy Straw Cleaner, developing an iphone application, and training for a half marathon seemed a bit much on my plate. There were many sleepless nights talking to China on the computer till the wee hours of the morning, and my kiddos had more chicken nuggets in those 4 months than they had had in their whole lifetime. I found that if I made lists and was able to complete one task before taking on others it helped me to focus more. I was never caught without having a spiral notebook in my hand.

What steps did you take to market your product? How did you determine the best route for you?

First and foremost, I believe that you must have a working website this day in age. Surprisingly, you don't have to pay big dollars for one though as expected. I think my website cost me $60 total. I owe just about every individual sale and almost all wholesale accounts to the amazing networking done through social media...ie Twitter, Facebook, and Mommy Bloggers. Being a mom and trying to launch a "mom" product, who better to chat with then other moms via the internet? I would suggest diving into social media with everything you've got.

Are there any lessons that your business has taught you?

Yes, absolutely nothing goes exactly how you planned it. There will be bumps in the road that you didn't foresee and you just deal with them as they come. Be open-minded and always ask for lots of feedback. Also, stay organized and document everything. If you haven't started an inventor's composition notebook, do so immediately and record every interaction that you make with people, products, and services.

FRONT   BACK

Is there any advice you'd like to share with fellow mom inventors that are just getting started?

I think it is imperative that you do tons of research on the internet before ever spending a penny. With the internet, Google specifically, you're able to research similar products on the market, patents, market analysis, and statistics pertaining to your invention. Also, I would get my hands on the Mom Inventors Handbook by Tamara Monosoff. This is an incredible resource that will take you through the entire invention process. I still use it almost daily.[22]

So while you may think that you are crazy to start a new venture or expand your business now, it's actually one of the best times you could choose. The barriers are historically relatively low.

Have you noticed that there is an opportunity and a market for absolutely everything these days? Pick any subject at all, Google it, and you are likely to get more than one response. If you were to have an idea that didn't return a lot of Google search results, chances are you've stumbled on to a potential opportunity. Where I live in the Northeast, it is possible to hire a service provider for almost everything you can think of. In addition to the usual handymen and house cleaners, there are even services you can call to come clean up the lawn after your dog has used it for his potty. There are freelancers of all types. I know of one woman who pays someone to open and sort her mail for her twice a month. There is an in-home laundry service in my area. I always wonder what they are doing in between wash cycles. Children's classes exist for just about every type of activity and skill that you might want your child to learn. You can even hire someone to teach your kid how to ride a bike without training wheels. Seriously, markets abound for just about anything, so your business likely has merit, even if you haven't yet hit your stride.

Use your sleepless nights to your advantage. Sleeping has never been a problem for me, so not being able to sleep during pregnancy was something new. I didn't let it upset me, though. I just turned those quiet hours into time to develop new ideas in my business. Harold Taylor, a notable expert in time management, takes a walk every morning to a local coffee shop, and once he is there, he writes an article. One holiday, his kids gave him an audio player so he could catch up on audio material during his walk. Everyone thought it was a good idea, until he realized his daily mental routine had been short circuited. Once he got to the coffee shop, he wasn't able to write his articles. They just weren't coming to him. He finally realized his downtime was the space his brain needed to create new thoughts.[23] I've experienced this myself a thousand times when I've thought of some absolutely clever thing to say only way after the excitement of some tense moment. Our minds need a little down time, and if we aren't getting it while sleeping, we can problem solve and plan in those dark hours.

What About the Economy?

You might hear people say that this is a crazy time to be in business. The fact is, the worst time to be in business is only when you can't be profitable. The absolute best time to be in business is when you are motivated and when you can do what you love. If this baby isn't the best reason ever to be in charge of your own life, there never will be a better reason.

I refer to my business as my first baby. I put in many hours during the first couple of years that I would not be able to invest now. It is ideal to have the kind of structure and support in your business that allows it to continue to grow while you are off having your baby. The fact is that in a troubled economy, if your business is strong, you might succeed where others won't. Especially if you know your numbers and have skills, talent and motivation, you can benefit from a shake out in the market, where weaker companies or less motivated business owners close their doors.

If you have an established business, you are able to ride the waves in any economy and exploit your company's edge. You likely have a customer base and experience that you can leverage to get you through a downturn. The trick is staying focused on the revenues and the reasons you are in business. If you haven't done a business plan in a while, now is a good time to revisit the basics. Read through Chapter 11 and do the exercises to ensure you are on track.

Depending on your market, you may find that stronger competitors can help you. Competitors may refer unwanted jobs to you. One real estate title search company has built an entire business out of being the company that gets called for problem searches. Or you may be able to provide subcontracting services to help other businesses with an overflow of work. A social services company provides respite care to mentally challenged adults and has been busy since the day they opened their doors with overflow work from other agencies. Most small business people are really just like you. They are made up of interesting people who are providing for their families, and they are willing to help you be successful. In fact, you may find your competitors are actually colleagues who are interested in having more service providers who can help grow the market for everyone. This is where being an excellent subcontractor or independent contractor might be an option for you.

Need another reason to use this economy as an excuse to be in business for yourself? Childcare savings. Who can really afford to pay for excellent childcare? Most American families get little or no assistance with expensive childcare costs. If you can arrange your schedule to reduce or eliminate childcare, you've just given yourself a raise. That is real money in your pocket. In economic terms, it's called opportunity cost. The opportunity cost of you providing your own childcare could be thousands, even tens of thousands of dollars each year. If you look at the numbers another way, that's less money you have to earn to have the same or better quality of life.

Retrain or retrench? Choose the latter. Have you ever noticed that when the economy is down, people go back to school in droves to improve their chances at getting a job? Ah, but you aren't competing for the jobs that companies offer. You can pave your own way to income, flexibility, and autonomy. Have a business plan. Work on your business, not just in it. By the time the economy swings again, you'll have a child and a business, or at least the experience that comes with both.

Education

Here you are sporting a basketball-sized belly, trying to get a handle on finances at home and in your businesses, bursting with creative ideas for the nursery, searching for the perfect childcare, and solving every problem you've ever encountered in your business. One temptation is to put off additional business training and education until after the baby comes, because it seems like there might be a lot of downtime in those weeks and maybe months after the little one arrives. For some reason, this ideal just didn't pan out for me, and I suspect it won't for you either. If there are crackerjack opportunities for you to pick up new tricks or hone your skills, your pregnancy window might just be the best window that you have. You'll probably never have this much time again.

There are a number of fabulous ways to make this work for you. If there is a trade show or annual conference that you've always wanted to attend, provided that you have your doctor's approval, go ahead and attend now. Take your partner, extend the trip a few days, and make this as much of a tax-deductible babymoon as you can. Be sure to check with your CPA on rules for deducting business travel.

If you can't or choose not to travel, check out industry related webinars and teleconferences, which are often free or given at very reasonable prices. All you need is a phone, sometimes an internet connection, and an hour or two in order to listen. If you aren't familiar with this type of distance learning, here are a few tips. Be sure to test your connection to the presentation host well in advance, so that you can work out any technology kinks ahead of time. Use a speaker phone or headphone to reduce stress to your neck, shoulders, and back. Know how to use your mute button to minimize background noise from your connection. Have a drink and snacks prepared ahead of time, if this will help keep you focused and in front of your computer. Need I remind you to take a pre-session potty break? Above all, resist the urge to multitask, especially if you are in front of your computer and especially if you have paid for the privilege of attending the session. If you are in a profession that requires continuing educational units (CEUs), be sure to keep a copy of the receipt, session description, and your notes as proof of your attendance, as well as any CEU certificate that may be provided to you.

As much as you'd like to think that you'll be able to attend this type of education post-baby, babies have a way of not sticking to their schedule and diverting your attention from any structured learning that you'll try to attend from home. So if there's been something you've been dying to learn, do it now, when the worst you'll have to deal with is extra bathroom breaks. This type of investment in yourself and in your business might just be what sets you apart in any economy.

Guidance for Those
Without a Business Yet

If you aren't already in business for yourself, and you are dreaming of a way to work from home, keep in mind that anything worth having takes time. While there are plenty of work-at-home moms (WAHMs), there are plenty of moms who don't run their business from home. You could start a retail store, establish an office in rented space, buy a franchise, or work as a subcontractor for others. Look for "Best Businesses" lists that websites and reputable magazines offer each year. Below is a sampling.

http://entrepreneurs.about.com/cs/businessideas/
a/10startupideas.htm

http://www.ehow.com/about_4577680_best-businesses-
women-start.html

http://www.inc.com/ss/best-industries-starting-business-
right-now

Industries evolve as trends and technologies do, so be sure to match your skills with today's opportunities. Hot opportunities may not meet your needs, including your income needs. These resources are a good place to start.

When you decide to be in business for yourself, you need to make a few key decisions. You'll need to decide on the business structure, which might be sole proprietorship, partnership, LLC, or corporation. This may seem a little dry, but it's a good idea to know these terms, because your choices have tax and legal implications. A sole proprietorship is easy to establish, usually requiring a simple and inexpensive registration with the county or other local municipality. A sole proprietorship is also appropriate for a husband and wife operating a business together, since they are viewed as a single unit in the business. A sole proprietor business model requires an honest look at risks, liabilities, and insurance coverage, as it does leave an individual open to more legal challenges and personal liability than other forms of business.

A partnership is also easy to establish. However, partnerships are often entered into by friends in a honeymoon period of their business idea. Consider at the beginning of the venture what would happen if things change, such as the business takes a loss or is devalued, one partner moves or wants to leave the business, or either partner wants to head in a different direction. A written plan covering the termination of the business might seem like writing the divorce papers before the wedding, but the reality is that it is just good business. Having a plan is especially important if one or both of the partners is pregnant or planning other lifestyle changes, as they might not be able to continue on with the same commitments to the business after a major life change. Although partnerships are easy to enter into, most business advisors warn against operating in a partnership business model, especially when an LLC or corporation is relatively easy to establish.

A corporation can be an S-Corp, C-Corp, or an LLC. Each form of a corporation has advantages in certain situations.

A corporation can include a single or multiple owners. There are certain tax and liability considerations that might steer you towards this type of business structure. It's best to do more research and talk to a business advisor, such as those you can talk with at the Small Business Administration (www.SBA.gov) or SCORE (www.SCORE.org) for more advice on what might be right for you.

A business can change forms during its lifespan. For example, many companies start as sole proprietorships and change to an LLC structure as they mature.

Remember that businesses exist to make money. You may truly have a passion for what you do, and you may believe that you want to help people with your talent, but running a failing business is like volunteering with a pay cut. From the start, look at the finances of the business, and perhaps enlist a helper if this isn't your strong suit. You want to look at possible barriers to entry, such as capital investment in facilities or inventories (even if that inventory is just your starter kit from Mary Kay Cosmetics), required licensing (such as state certifications to practice accounting), and facilities (even if the facility is going to be your spare bedroom). Some businesses really can be run from the kitchen table for a while or forever. Do your due diligence, and then revisit your plan yearly to make sure you are on track.

Are you crazy to be in business for yourself? Absolutely not! You can be your own boss, have unlimited income potential, earn tax benefits unheard of by most employees, satisfy a market need, and possibly build an enterprise that could outlive you. If you have no one else to encourage you that you are on the right track, then let me tell you again that business ownership is an asset for you.

Critical Questions:

- Are you doing what you love? If not, how can you adjust your business?

- Are you taking advantage of the non-financial benefits most important to you?

- Are you leveraging all of your past experience and expertise?

- Do you have an idea that you would like to bring to market? If so, what steps would you need to take to do that?

- How can you leverage the current economic conditions to strengthen your business?

- Are there educational opportunities that you could take advantage of before the baby comes?

- If you don't yet have a business, can you identify one place or resource, one person, and one book you can learn from in the next week that would help you decide what business to open?

Taking Care of You: Run Your Business without Running Yourself Ragged

Any basic pregnancy book is going to give you a month-by-month list of symptoms and phenomenon that you might experience. Although experiences can be generalized, every woman is unique, and sometimes the same woman can have radically different pregnancies. One thing that you might experience is the variation in energy cycles in each trimester. My own experience was that each trimester, almost down to the week, my energy level changed dramatically. You may never fully plan for your particular pregnancy outcome, but you can prepare, and that may make all the difference in how you feel about your pregnancy, your business, and your life.

First Trimester

During the first trimester, sleep is imperative. In fact, exhaustion may be one of the first signs of your pregnancy. It's hard to believe that such a small thing can be such a drag on your body already, even before anyone else is able to discern anything unusual, and way before you start sporting a new shape. Amazing but true. After all, you are making eyelashes! Your body is doing something new, creating a whole new person out of the resources you already have on board. Once you find out the happy news, you may thank your lucky stars that you are in business for yourself. Sometimes, certainly not always, you may be able to schedule yourself to catch those extra Z's. Sleep later in the morning or schedule in naps once in a while. A corporate boss wouldn't usually look kindly on a little creative interpretation of your schedule, but if you are the boss, you might be able to swing it. If you schedule your own appointments, take advantage. This is really important in the first trimester, and the need usually decreases in the second trimester.

If you've always eaten a healthy diet, congratulations. You may need just a quick primer on a solid pregnancy diet to give your little one an extra boost of the good stuff. If, however, your lunches are burgers and fries or a snack bar and a soda, plan on making some adjustments. With baby on board, you don't need to eat two portions of everything. Your baby is getting snack sized versions of whatever you are eating, so you need to eat the right amount of the good stuff. Not only do you want to ensure your little one is getting enough nutrition, you also might want to consider the research that says that babies get acclimated to tastes they experience in utero, and they are more likely to prefer those tastes as youngsters. This makes a very good case for exposing your baby to fruits and vegetables way before his or her first solid foods at about six months.

Even at this early stage, stress is something you want to minimize. You may not be sleeping well with all of the planning and possibilities that run through your mind. Your hormones and state of mind contribute to your overall health, which can contribute to your baby's health. In other words, don't stress about things you don't need to. Preparation on the home front and in the business should be underway, but details might take months to work out. You see this freak-out factor going on when someone in her second or third month of pregnancy is zapping everything in the baby superstore for her registry. You may not have picked out names yet. You probably won't have fully thought through or researched all of your childcare options. And all of this is OK. Instead, concentrate on the big picture questions, like:

- Are we in the right sized home or apartment for our family?
- Are we happy with where we live and the jobs we have?
- What changes have I wanted to make in my business that I should act on right now?

These big picture questions will start to filter down to more detail-oriented questions over the next three months or so. Start your research. Learn what you need to, not the whole shebang. For instance, you might want to learn about daycare options in your area, but you don't need to complete a tour of all the facilities in a twenty mile radius just yet. If you are a planner, you can sign up for birth preparation classes, but don't freak out if you and your partner have never actually diapered a baby. Reality check: you don't need diapering skills just yet.

One thing you should do right away, as soon as you suspect you are pregnant, is see your doctor or healthcare provider. If you have a relationship with an OB/GYN that you like, head there first. Even if you come up with a plus sign on the home pregnancy kit, you'll want to get this first visit lined up as soon as you can. This will start you down the path of blood work, evaluation for any known risks, more learning opportunities, and from time to time, free stuff offered through doctors offices. You just became a demographer's dream, so there will be free samples and coupons for the asking.

If you live in an area with multiple hospitals, you may never have thought to ask which hospital your OB/GYN is associated with. Your doctor's privileges may dictate which hospital you can go to for delivery, so that might make one less decision for you to make. If you wish to deliver at a different hospital, because of proximity, reputation, or facilities, decide as early as possible whether your doctor can accommodate you or if you'll need to switch providers.

This early stage is also a good time to investigate whether you might want to break from traditional medicine and head down the path of midwifery. If you make this decision, it may take some time to find resources in your area, although this specialty is making a comeback. You can find more through the American Association of Birth Centers (www. BirthCenters.org) and other resources available on the internet related to midwifery. Because you are likely to need only monthly checkups through your sixth month, you only have a few opportunities to see your provider and make a choice about your care early on. Talk with colleagues, friends, and family about their experiences.

It might seem like there is a lot to get done, but of course, the rest of your life goes on. You may feel like an imposter at this point if you decide not to disclose your situation right away to friends and colleagues. Do what seems right for you. Don't feel pressured to start making excuses for meal choices, doctor appointments, or time for rest. Simply state only the needed facts (as in, I am really trying to eat healthier these days), and leave it at that. Especially if you are in the advanced maternal age category, you may decide to keep your news quiet for the first three months when the risk of miscarriage is highest.

Second Trimester

My second trimester started at exactly fourteen weeks, and it was like a light switch had been flipped. I suddenly wasn't tired anymore, I was in the middle of my busy season at work and picking up three new clients each week, and I was back to sleeping well. This burst of energy is often reported, but it isn't a sure thing. While you may have more energy, you might not have the strength or grace you had just a few weeks ago as your shape starts to change.

The second trimester (fourteen to twenty-seven weeks) is the time to get things done. Plan ahead. Travel. Attend your favorite annual conferences. Hire an assistant. Join networking groups. Do some long range planning with your partner. Be careful not to overdo it, and remember that taking care of your little one means taking care of you. Maintain a nutritious eating routine.

Probably one of the most fun things you can do is arrange and take a babymoon with your partner. It might be a challenge to get away, especially if you are juggling two hectic schedules, but this will probably be the best time in your life to do it. You have the flexibility to schedule yourself out, you feel healthy, you probably even have that pregnant glow, and you aren't lugging around an unpredictable baby or baby gear. Although your partner may not realize it yet, this may be the best opportunity you have to make him feel special since, in just a few weeks, all eyes are going to turn to your expanding belly and then the new baby.

Third Trimester

The third trimester again seemed to turn on a dime for me. At exactly twenty-eight weeks, I started to feel sluggish, huge and exhausted again. Although I had put several new business ideas on the planning boards, I worried about how to get them all off the ground so they'd be working well during and after my maternity leave. The third trimester feels like a snowball gathering speed as it heads downhill, so this is a time to start phasing out activities, not to add huge new projects, unless you are fortunate enough to have staff to be able to carry them through.

Sleep and rest again become important. My own experience was that even though I needed more sleep, my physical discomforts prevented me from getting a solid night of sleep. You'll start to feel your baby kick during the third trimester. If your baby has his or her own little Riverdance routine worked out, you might be kept up late or woken up early. Again, good nutrition at the right times of day can help to balance out the baby and make his or her cohabitation something to make you smile.

Pregnancy calendars give you forty to forty-two weeks for full gestation, but early in the third trimester you should prepare for the unexpected, which may mean taking leave earlier than you might have thought. Prepare not only with a traditional bag packed ready for the hospital, but also with contingency plans with clients, staff, and coworkers. If only you have the figurative or literal keys to the kingdom, consider whether you need to allow someone else access to critical information (bank accounts, email accounts, key client contacts, passwords) should you suddenly be sentenced to bed rest or early labor and delivery. Will you be scheduling meetings right up until the last minute? I remember scheduling with a new client just two weeks before my due date. I created a contingency plan with him before our first meeting, so he would be aware if I were to go into labor that I would not be calling him to cancel our scheduled appointment. Most people are quite wonderful, and with appropriate information, they are accommodating in ways you might not expect.

Case Study

Kristy is in the business of taking care of others, but she took some significant steps to take care of herself when she was pregnant. She is an accomplished aesthetician with a good reputation and a stable client following at an established salon. She always dreamed of being self-employed, sparked by her entrepreneur parents. While she was preparing for their second child, she and her husband started scenario planning for their ideal business. With an eighteen-month-old at home, and another on the way, she wasn't sure that her current employer would be flexible enough for her family, and she couldn't afford to not work at all. Her decision to transform into a business owner became easier when her employer upended her schedule and cut her work hours just days before she was due to return after maternity leave.

Having been in research mode while she was pregnant, she was able to quickly knit together the details and have her own wellness spa under lease arrangements just three months after her son was born. This all happened in the midst of the Great Recession. Since her husband was also between jobs, he dove in to support the back-office of the business. They rent a highly visible retail location and have a permanent staff that includes hair stylists, massage therapists, aestheticians, and receptionists.

Her experience of working for others drives her desire to create a business that is based on trust, confidence, excellence, and the human touch. She hires staff who love what they do, and they make each client feel special. In a very crowded market, Kristy knows that her spa is financially profitable and sustainable for the next five years and more. Although she and her husband have built a self-financed business, she operates with all the financial rigor that she would have if a bank were holding her note. When it comes to women in business, she feels that confidence is the backbone to success, and she encourages other women to develop their confidence in their own field. Owning her own business allows Kristy a better quality of life with her family, avoiding traditional daycare and allowing her to participate in her children's daytime activities. Maybe ready access to massages and organic spa treatments isn't a cure-all, but it sure hasn't hurt her ability to keep moving forward.

Nutrition

When it comes to nutrition for you and the baby, common sense prevails. Unfortunately, our country has become disconnected from farming, and not everyone has good nutrition education. The best advice for anyone, including pregnant women, comes from Michael Pollan, author of *Food Rules: An Eater's Manual.* His advice is only seven words, "Eat real food, mostly plants, not too much."[24] He means you want to reduce or eliminate processed foods, and eat a diet that consists of protein and carbohydrates and even fats, since all are needed to fuel our bodies.

Heidi Murkoff offers up "The Pregnancy Diet" in *What to Expect When You're Expecting.* This is a great list of guidelines to get you through your meals. She even goes so far as to offer the "Pregnancy Daily Dozen." Unfortunately, as great as it is,

I could never bring myself to count whether I had satisfied the dozen or not. But after reading through the advice, it still adds up to, "Eat real food, mostly plants, not too much." The most interesting thing is that calorie requirements for a baby on board are much lower than one might think. You only need an additional three hundred calories a day, which can be consumed in just one or two extra high quality snacks. More than this and you'll be wearing that great new maternity wardrobe for much longer than you planned. So while you don't need to double up on the groceries in the company fridge, you do want to spend as much time strategizing on healthy options as you spend ordering office supplies. That extra candy bar might provide the calories, but not the nutrition your baby needs.

The Pregnancy Daily Dozen Summary[25]

Calories	Approximately 300 additional high-quality calories daily
Protein	3 servings daily
Calcium	4 servings daily
Vitamin C foods	3 servings daily
Green leafy and yellow vegetables and yellow fruits	3-4 servings daily
Other fruits and vegetables	1-2 servings daily
Whole grains and legumes	6 or more servings daily
Iron-rich foods	Some daily
Fats and high-fat food	Approximately 4 servings daily (depending on your weight gain)
Salty foods	In moderation
Fluids	At least eight 8-oz glasses daily
Prenatal vitamin supplement	A pregnancy formula taken daily

I try to live by the adage, "All things in moderation," but when it comes to foods for the pregnant lady, there are some things you should steer clear of. Sushi is out. Cold cut meats harbor bacteria that you don't want to pass on to your baby. Caffeine should be limited to one cup of coffee or less each day, although I know plenty of women who drank coffee throughout their pregnancies. Don't even think about alcohol. Despite what your mother may have done when she was pregnant with you, we know there is a real risk to fetuses, and that glass of wine is just not worth the risk. This is the one area that might give you away in a business situation if you are used to schmoozing with a drink in your hand. Be prepared with a cover story if you aren't ready to share the news but you are at a function where someone might notice your abstinence. You can always say you are dieting, and you're cutting out those high calorie cocktails for just a bit.

You might get lucky, like I did with my first baby, who decided she didn't like any kind of sweets. Despite my normally raging sweet tooth, I didn't touch a cookie, cake or candy for nine months. Perhaps that is part of the reason she is still an excellent eater even as a toddler.

Food is everywhere in our culture, but it is often highly processed and packaged for a long shelf life. Busy business people often feel like we get caught without healthy options. Make a few key changes in your schedule and you can confidently eat for the two of you. Simple changes like tossing frozen chicken breasts in the slow cooker in the morning before you leave for appointments mean you have your main dish ready to go when you might be too tired to think about cooking after 5 p.m. Accompanied by some veggies from the freezer and some rice or stuffing, you have a healthy, no fuss meal. Get in the habit of packing a few pieces of fruit on appointments that might run through mid-day. If you have food with you, you are less likely to make poor decisions at a drive-through. Show some willpower at the grocery store so you don't have to struggle at home when you are at your weakest. If chips and fried foods don't make it into your grocery cart, they won't be on the pantry shelves to sabotage your day. If you have access to a community supported agriculture co-op (CSA) or farm market, schedule yourself an appointment each week to visit and pick up fresh produce. You can find CSAs at www.LocalHarvest.org. You are more likely to actually use it if you make a special effort to get it. My favorite cookbook, even after pregnancy, is still *Eating Well When You're Expecting*,[26] also by Heidi Murkoff and Sharon Mazel. The recipes in that book are yummy and flavorful versions of old standbys.

Outsource if you are too busy to cook. You might be able to bring in a personal chef. It might sound like an extravagance, but it might not be as much of a splurge as you think. If you are already eating out much or all of the time, the cost of a personal chef will be roughly comparable to takeout. Having someone work with you means they can customize dishes to your taste and dietary needs. If a professional isn't the answer, see how much your partner is willing to help out with food prep. You might be surprised.

Right about now you might be wondering about the race towards organic. Should you be buying organic food? Is it worth the price? Can you afford it? Can you afford not to? It is unfortunate that we've gotten to the point where we know which foods are better for us, but the food industry makes unhealthy, processed food more available and more affordable. Mr. Pollan's food mantra makes sense, "Eat real food, mostly plants, not too much." If you want to eat organic items but you are on a limited budget, you can check out the Dirty Dozen and the Clean Fifteen Shoppers Guide from the Environmental Working Group.[27] This was created to help guide consumers in their choices to reducing pesticides in their diets, which is something to consider, especially when pregnant. However, it's best not to lose your common sense on this topic. A regular old non-organic apple is pretty much always going to be a better bet than the super-sized order of

French fries. If you can make these choices for you and your baby now, you'll have lots of practice when it comes to feeding your baby food when she's sitting at the table in about a year.

Environmental Working Group
The Power of Information
Headquarters 1436 U St. N.W.,
Suite 100
Washington, DC 20009
(202) 667-6982

Why Should You Care About Pesticides?
The growing consensus among scientists is that small doses of pesticides and other chemicals can cause lasting damage to human health, especially during fetal development and early childhood. Scientists now know enough about the long-term consequences of ingesting these powerful chemicals to advise that we minimize our consumption of pesticides.

What's the Difference?
EWG research has found that people who eat five fruits and vegetables a day from the Dirty Dozen list consume an average of 10 pesticides a day. Those who eat from the 15 least contaminated conventionally-grown fruits and vegetables ingest fewer than 2 pesticides daily. The Guide helps consumers make informed choices to lower their dietary pesticide load.

Will Washing and Peeling Help?
The data used to create these lists is based on produce tested as it is typically eaten (meaning washed, rinsed or peeled, depending on the type of produce). Rinsing reduces but does not eliminate pesticides. Peeling helps, but valuable nutrients often go down the drain with the skin. The best approach: eat a varied diet, rinse all produce and buy organic when possible.

How Was This Guide Developed?
EWG analysts have developed the Guide based on data from nearly 96,000 tests for pesticide residues in produce conducted between 2000 and 2008 and collected by the U.S. Department of Agriculture and the U.S. Food and Drug Administration. You can find a detailed description of the criteria EWG used to develop these rankings and the complete list of fruits and vegetables tested at our dedicated website, www.foodnews.org

Physical Limitations

When planning your work, your changing energy levels, physical shape, and physical condition may have you modifying activities that you've always taken for granted. As in all things, moderation is the key. One thing I didn't expect is how balance is affected, sometimes way earlier than expected. In part, this can be due to the naturally occurring hormone relaxin, which starts to loosen up your joints and ligaments almost the instant you become pregnant. Normally a fairly graceful person, I started turning my ankles even on flat, solid ground. Sports and activities that aren't actually forbidden during pregnancy may still not be as enjoyable. I didn't like being on my bicycle past four months. Work activities that you never thought twice about may now be just downright unpleasant. During my pregnancy my tolerance for hot spaces and standing in line was really low. You may find that your environment requires you to rethink your approach to some of your work as well.

Most activities can be safely continued right up to your delivery as long as you are in good health. In my line of work, I routinely lift and haul moderately heavy loads around work sites. I am also on ladders, and I install some shelving for clients. In fact, I was still installing for clients well into my ninth month, although the process did require caution and a bit more time to complete. I also took the precaution of only being on a ladder with someone else present, just in case.

Others may have old fashioned ideas about your abilities during your pregnancy and what a pregnant woman shouldn't do. Be sure to check with your health care provider about specific recommendations based on your health, your baby's health, and your work environment. In general, however, it is recognized that a woman should stay active and moving in order to remain healthy, which can contribute to an easier delivery and recovery. Whenever clients expressed concern about my physical exertion, I would thank them for their concern and then say, "As much as I enjoy working with you, my baby is my top concern, and I would absolutely request help rather than take any risk with her." This usually put clients at ease that I was a professional who was going to use care and common sense.

Save your energy. Take help when it is offered, even if this isn't easy for you. Sit if you don't have to stand. Lie down if you don't have to sit. Exercise when you feel up to it, but not within three hours before bedtime. Walking and swimming are two great exercises that don't require an investment or special training, and both provide great aerobic benefits. Sleep when you can, because your body needs that rest to make amazing little baby parts, like a button nose and toenails. Avoid caffeine and heavy meals before bed. Stick to a regular sleep routine, adding massage or aromatherapy if they are helpful.

Some of the same things that are good for you are really good for your baby and your business. According to Richard Nisbett in his book, *Intelligence and How to Get It*, "So you haven't wasted your time, money and patience on your children after all. If you were to average the contribution of genetics to IQ over different social classes, you would probably find 50 percent to be the maximum contribution of genetics."[28] Throughout his book, he posits that the effort that goes into raising children and providing them with rich and diverse experiences helps to bring about a higher level of IQ and a greater level of overall intelligence. In fact, the subtitle of his book is, *Why Schools and Cultures Count*. His basic premise is that there are definite factors, beyond the genetic explanations provided in the classic texts, that can be controlled for greater intelligence, and therefore better life experiences. The most interesting is Nisbett's statement that, "Bigger babies grow up to be smarter adults than do smaller babies…Women who exercise on a treadmill twenty minutes a day a few times a week have bigger babies, and bigger babies are certainly healthier and may well grow up to be smarter because of some variable associated with their size. That variable could be brain size. Babies born to exercising mothers have larger heads. We know that people with larger brains are more intelligent on average."[29] In short, women who exercise tend to have bigger babies who have bigger heads, which may lead to higher IQs. Even if this isn't an undeniably proven fact, exercise is good for you and the baby, and everybody else for that matter. Listen to your doctor. Make time for some regular form of exercise, even if it is just a walk through your neighborhood. Like a prenatal vitamin, it is something very simple that could make a significant difference in the health of both of you.

Books are good. It turns out that being read to and exposure to books are socio-economic indicators that are found with higher-IQ children according to Nisbett.[30] Earlier and more consistent access to schools and learning programs are also highly correlated with higher intelligence.[31] Being exposed to the problem solving, like that required to run a successful business, must qualify as educational, rich, and diverse experiences. Entrepreneurial mothers were not highlighted as a group in *Intelligence and How to Get It*. Although not scientifically studied, it makes sense that if you are steeped in the entrepreneurial environment and, even better, expose your child to aspects of it, your child is likely to benefit cognitively from that experience.

Safety

As long as we're talking about taking care of you, let's not forget safety. As a woman, there are basic security measures you might have in place in business. However, you may feel more at risk because you are now worrying for two. If your business requires you to visit clients in their homes or businesses, there are security measures you can take, which may include:

- Only taking business from sources you know, such as past clients
- Conducting a phone interview before an on-site meeting

- Ensuring that you have an assistant or partner on appointments
- Providing another party with a record of your appointment location and contact
- Never agreeing to a meeting alone in an out-of-the-way location or at odd hours
- Setting up a call-in system for arriving at and departing from the client location
- Limiting your clients to a certain geography or other criteria

The vast majority of people are good and trustworthy, but there is no reason at all to put yourself and your unborn child in danger. If the hairs on the back of your neck go up, it is probably for good reason. It is better to arrive at a client location, only to drive away without introduction, if you feel unsafe. While you may lose one client, your safety is paramount. Even firefighters, EMTs, and first responders are taught to take care of number one before offering help to another. You are no help to anyone, let alone the baby on board, if you are injured or threatened.

Side Effects and Symptoms

You can find a list of weird pregnancy side effects and symptoms in *What to Expect When You're Expecting* or one of the many pregnancy websites. You have no real way to know what pregnancy prize package you are going to win. Some of the symptoms show up pretty reliably at a certain number of weeks, and some never do, thankfully. Here is a partial list just to give you an idea:

- Mommy brain is what we call any lapses in memory or judgment that you care to blame on your little freeloader.
- Vision changes start to occur, especially if you wear contacts or glasses, around three months. I stopped wearing my contact lenses for several months. Your vision

and prescription is likely to return to normal after the baby arrives, as mine did.

- Morning sickness may not happen to you, but if it does, I recommend chewing on some candied ginger. While this is a little hot for my taste, it kept the queasies at bay for me. Since morning sickness can happen any time of the day, or the entire day for days at a time, this might disrupt your ability to focus and function.

- Bad backs are just par for the course. The best defense against a bad back is a strong abdominal core, which means doing proper crunches and other stabilizing exercises before you are pregnant. Once you get pregnant, your abs literally separate from each other, so sit ups are a no-no after about the third month. They will mend after the birth, but it takes a while.

- Bad feet and swollen ankles can show up around the sixth or seventh month, right about when you'll be taking your babymoon, so plan to rest often, with your feet elevated as much as possible. And although it seems like you are holding water in your ankles, oddly flushing your body by drinking lots of water is one of the best ways to prevent swelling.

- Incontinence is all too common for women during pregnancy and after. Find out what a Kegel is and start doing them now.

- Gas, constipation, and bloating...but you were expecting these, right? Reduce or eliminate fatty foods. Some vegetables like cabbage may exacerbate the problem, but don't nix all the good veggies from your diet, because they keep things running regular, if you know what I mean.

- Hair and nails take on a different tone. Usually hair gets stronger and thicker, but you'll lose it about three months after the baby is born, and it is all due to the hormones that you two share. You may find nails are stronger and grow more quickly.

- Skin either clears up or develops acne, but either way, wash in a mild soap like Dove or Cetaphil. You may also develop skin tags, which are random little flaps of skin on your arms or other places that may or may not go away after the baby comes, but a dermatologist can remove them.

I developed a pyogenic granuloma on my hand, although they can develop elsewhere like the mouth. It was basically a small blood vessel that burst through the skin, and had to be cauterized by a dermatologist.

- Heat and cold sensitivity goes on overdrive. Since you may feel like you have a Crock-Pot® strapped to your tummy, you are likely to be hotter all the time, which is great in February but not so much in August. Just remember, in August everyone is hot and slow, not just the pregnant ladies.

This is by no means a complete list, but just the top few. You can think about how any or all of these might affect the work that you do, and see if it would cause mild or major inconvenience in your daily routine.

About Him

Not only should you take care of you and the little one inside, but you'll want to remember to take care of your partner. He's the reason you are in this situation, after all. What you might not know is that he's pregnant, too. That's right, it turns out that while all of your hormones are going haywire, so are his, as reported by *Scientific American*.[32] He's likely to be experiencing mood swings and emotions on a scale that he doesn't normally experience thanks to a condition called couvade, or sympathetic pregnancy. Of course, guys handle their emotions differently than women, but it helps to know that he really is along for the ride and is not just a passive observer. He also might, despite his best intentions, be struggling with irrational thoughts, like whether you will love the baby more than him.

This is an excellent time to plan some alone time, even at the expense of the business. I know, you are thinking that you can't get away, or he can't get away. But in a couple of years, it is likely that you won't get any closer to the Caribbean than cruise commercials on TV. So book your trip now. When we got pregnant, we decided to finally take the trip to Paris that we had been dreaming of for over ten years. However, my maternal instincts were in overdrive by month six, and world events had me second guessing overseas travel safety. So instead of the Eiffel Tower and Notre Dame, we settled for an extended weekend in Quebec City, just a short plane ride north to Canada. We had a wonderful, romantic weekend in a castle, but Paris has gone on the back burner again until our girls are able to order their own crepes by asking for them in French. If you have big decisions that you are still trying to work out, like how long of a leave you are planning on taking from your jobs, a babymoon might be just the right time to come to agreement on them. Get his support on things that you are still noodling through, and maybe you'll get more of that sleep that you desperately need.

Critical Questions:

- Have you settled on the type of care and birth facility you plan to use?

- What adjustments do you need to make to your diet, and do you need help or support?

- Are there physical aspects of your work that will require modification?

- Are there things you can do, like exercise and attending cultural activities, which you feel would be beneficial for your unborn baby?

- How can you support your partner now, so that he can best support you throughout the pregnancy?

Dress the Part

When I was pregnant for the first time, I remember very clearly one of my biggest questions to my doctor: how many different sizes of bras would I need? She was a wonderful doctor with lots of skill and empathy, but the poor woman just looked at me blankly and said she had no idea. I wasn't so much concerned with vanity as I was with the added wardrobe expense that was to come. I already had an entire closet full of clothes which fit me very well, and now I was going to have to pack them all away and buy entirely new ones? Yikes.

My first time in a Motherhood Maternity store was a joke. I was already feeling squeezed out of many of my regular clothes, and I was desperate to wear cute maternity tops to show the world that I was part of Club Motherhood, but nothing really fit yet. I had no way of guessing how big I might get, never having been pregnant before. After trying on four shirts that were all size medium but fit in wildly different extremes, the sales clerk and I agreed that pregnancy clothes had the same problems that regular clothes had, and were not reliably sized.

Since my weight normally doesn't fluctuate, I had no idea what an additional twenty pounds might look like on me. Actually, I ended up gaining forty pounds with each of my babies. In the middle of my first pregnancy, the Institute of Medicine issued new recommended weight gain charts, which are summarized on the following page: [33]

TABLE 1 NEW RECOMMENDATIONS FOR TOTAL AND RATE OF WEIGHT GAIN DURING PREGNANCY, BY PREPREGNANCY BMI

Pregnancy BMI	BMI+(kg/m²) (WHO)	Total Weight Gain Range (lbs)	Rates of Weight Gain* 2nd and 3rd Trimester (Mean Range in lbs / wk)
Underweight	<18.5	28–40	1 (1–1.3)
Normal Weight	18.5 - 24.9	25–35	1 (0.8–1)
Overweight	25.0 - 29.9	15–25	0.6 (0.5– 0.7)
Obese (includes all classes)	≥30.0	11–20	0.5 (0.4–0.6)

+ To calculate BMI go to www.nhlbisupport.com/bmi/
*Calculations assume a 0.5–2 kg (1.1–4.4 lbs) weight gain in the first trimester (based on Siga-Riz et al., 1994; Carmichael et al., 1997)

Even after seeing these charts, it's a good bet you still won't know exactly what to buy or where to shop. Let's talk about your sources first. There are five main places to get your maternity wear:

1. Retail shops like Motherhood Maternity, Wal-Mart, Target, and Babies"R"Us.

2. Maternity specialty sources, like those found in pregnancy catalogs and online. Since the relative market for these retailers is small, you'll have to search for these.

3. Thrift/consignment stores. Many children's thrift and consignment stores also have maternity sections. National stores like Goodwill Industries sometimes have maternity clothes, although they may not be in a dedicated section.

4. Borrowing might not be something you would do for your everyday clothes, but your sister and girlfriends are going to save you a lot of money if they are willing to pass along parts or all of their maternity wardrobe.

5. Swap options, like Freecycle.org and Freepeats.org. There are sites like this starting up every day, so do a little searching on the internet. These sites allow

you to offer or request useful items, often without
any money involved. If taking clothes from strangers
sounds bizarre, add up the savings to be had from a
completely or nearly free wardrobe that's new-to-you,
and you might change your tune.

Although every article on maternity dressing is going to offer
up your man's clothes as a budget saver, most of his gear, if it
does fit you, is not going to fit into your professional image. So
leave his clothes in his closet and hunt some for yourself.

What about those bras? Yes, the bras will probably be the
first to need an upgrade, so to speak. In fact, you are likely to
need to buy a new set of bras almost immediately (or at least it
seems that way), and then one or two more sets as you reach the
finish line. I fudged a little and purchased some bra extenders
from JoAnn Fabric & Craft stores (they were something like
two for a dollar), that allowed me to just add an inch or so to
the back of my current bras. As you get closer to the end of
your pregnancy, you'll want to have a good sense of whether
you intend to breastfeed your baby because, if you didn't know
before, there are bras made just for that task, and you'll want
those on hand if you decide to nurse. The shopkeepers seem to
hide these less than beautiful bras, but since they otherwise do
the same job as regular bras, you can make the last set of bras
you buy toward the end of your pregnancy be nursing bras.
Here's a timeline of what to buy and when for your girls:

Months 1-3	You can probably get away with your current duds.
Months 4-6	You'll probably need to trade up a model, but regular fashion will still work.
Months 7-9	You may need a maternity bra for extra support, because this is when you'll start to feel super-sized.

Post-baby	Your goals- support and easy access. Special nursing bras have front flaps that fold down for nursing. Skip anything with underwires to avoid clogged ducts while nursing.
Post-baby	Even after you quit nursing, you may not be back to your regular size. Welcome to the new normal.
Sleep tight	Skip sleeping in your bras at night and buy cheap, fitted tank tops or workout tanks if you need night time support.

34

Like everything else in business, it is nice to start with a budget for your maternity wardrobe, or at least a rough estimate of one. You can find maternity clothes that are reasonably priced, but I've found the quality of maternity clothes is pretty poor in general. Even if they aren't too pricey, if you were to buy a full wardrobe all at once, it would add up to a small fortune. By shopping almost exclusively at thrift and discount stores, I spent just $220 on a complete wardrobe. I don't work in an office, and therefore I don't see the same people day after day. I only needed a handful of professional outfits that I could stagger for the days at client sites. Here are some tricks I used to extend my wardrobe until I could finally pack it all away and get back to my real clothes.

Necessities

- Pants come first. They are the first thing you grow out of, and there is very little you can do to stay in those jeans. It happens quickly for the first pregnancy, and even more quickly for the second thanks to the body's muscle memory. You may find you need something bigger than your regular pants but not quite maternity pants for a few months. Belly bands, which are supposed to extend the life of your favorite pair of pants, did not work because they don't provide enough support for an active person who is lifting weight. The frugal trick of looping a rubber band over the button on my jeans never felt like a secure

95

option, either. Opt for non-maternity pants with elastic or drawstring tops to get you through this awkward period.

- Bra extenders, which can be found at craft stores like JoAnn Fabric & Craft stores, should be issued at every OB/GYN office. They aren't the end answer, but they'll buy you some time with your current undies.

- Great accessories should be the third part of your maternity wardrobe. A beautiful scarf, necklace, or bracelet is going to be something you can wear with many outfits, and will last way past your maternity gear. Never underestimate the power of a stylish accessory.

- Longer tops are great pieces to add to your wardrobe before you have to settle into maternity wear. It would seem like shirts that are loose would be wearable as you get bigger, but it turns out the length is more important than the width. A longer shirt provides better belly coverage and allows room to ride-up when it's needed. If you can find T-shirts in a longer length, they become great layering pieces that you can use with true maternity sweaters, jackets and blouses in colder seasons.

Shoes

- Lower your heel height, because even if you are used to high heels normally, your balance is going to be affected by hormones and your changing shape. Falling off your shoes isn't pretty and just isn't cool.

- Prepare for expansion, since feet typically grow a size, and sometimes two. Sometimes feet will return to their previous size, but not always.

- If you are lucky enough to be pregnant during the summer, you might find yourself just going without shoes most of the time, but you'll likely need some shoes for work. Spend the few extra bucks to find summer shoes that provide support; flips flops are for kids, not mature feet.

Wardrobe Strategies

- Stay professional, but you may as well have some fun with this wardrobe. I decided I wasn't buying any maternity top that didn't have sparkles or satin trim. I refused to wear plump versions of suits, and I nixed any options that were navy or brown. As this tiny alien changes your shape, there may be days you just don't feel pretty, so only buy clothes that you adore on the hanger, and you'll have a better chance of loving it on a bad hair day.

- Conventional wisdom says buy pieces in your basic colors so you can mix and match. Buy a few staples, like multiple pairs of black pants, but I say jazz up the rest with really pretty patterns and accent fabrics. This is the last time you'll wear silk for a while, because after the baby is born, silk won't stand up to the damage a newborn can do to a wardrobe. Sequined tops work now, but are too scratchy to wear when you are snuggling your newborn.

- Buy for the current season. You are likely to start wearing maternity clothes between month three and five, and you'll be pregnant another four to six months. But then, you may be wearing those same clothes on the way back down to your regular weight, which might take a few more months. Don't immediately buy clothes you think you'll be wearing when you are eight months pregnant. It's just too hard to plan ahead for your size and the weather, when both are hard to forecast.

- Choose lighter fabrics than you might normally, because you are likely to be warmer as you incubate your little one. When my second daughter was one year old, I was surprised to realize that I owned only five sweaters. After being pregnant and nursing for a few years in a row, my sweater supply had dwindled to next to nothing because I had been so warm while incubating and nesting.

- Dresses are a great wardrobe addition, since they are comfortable and can be dressed up or down with accessories. If you go for longer lengths, you might be able to eliminate the need for hosiery, depending on your industry. You might find that compression stockings help with ankle swelling, and you might be able to hide them under longer length skirts and dresses. However, unless they are specifically designed for the nursing mom, dresses are almost completely useless post-baby if you nurse. Top-and-bottom combos provide better nursing access. Still, it was worth it to have a few dresses during pregnancy that I didn't have to think about mixing or matching with anything except accessories.

- Blazers will work for a while, unbuttoned, but eventually you may find they get tight in the shoulders. Yep, the baby is adding bulk to your middle, but those extra pounds end up in strange places, like your shoulders.

- Remember that very few people walk out of the hospital wearing their old clothes. You might be wearing your maternity clothes for another three to nine months, so purchase things you can stand to wear for a while.

- Get one really, really great outfit. If you are in business, chances are you'll go to at least one event where you'll need to be dressed up. Don't miss out because you have nothing to wear. If you do any public speaking, you deserve to present yourself just as well when you are pregnant as you would any other time. In fact, the venue may require it.

- If you have a pretty solid idea that this will not be your last pregnancy, you can justify purchasing some additional or better quality items. However, keep in mind that nothing is guaranteed, and you may or may not get more than one season out of your wardrobe.

- On the flip side, if you are purchasing a wardrobe as opposed to borrowing, you have the right to make purchases for your benefit and body type, without regard to other friends or family who might want to borrow your wardrobe later if they also get pregnant. Women tend to be caretakers and givers by nature, but you need not try to care for a sister, cousin or friend who might be trying to get pregnant at the same time. Go ahead and make your choices for you, and don't worry about whether your sister would wear it.

Building a nearly complete second wardrobe will start to eat up your discretionary funds almost immediately. Start budgeting for it when you map out your finances for the next months. I am a huge fan of debt-free living, so I try to spend only cash on consumable things like clothes before purchases attack my credit cards. When I built my maternity wardrobe, my strategy was to allow myself to use any remaining cash I had in my wallet at the end of the week for a new maternity outfit. This assured that I was able to transition through the seasons with new clothes as needed, and that I wasn't creating a debt that I could have otherwise used for essential (and longer lasting) baby gear.

Maternity clothes were not my favorite aspect of my pregnancies. Most people I know just went for a sensible wardrobe that got them by. That is a fine strategy, but as a professional and an entrepreneur, don't forget to present yourself professionally. Invest in a wardrobe that allows you to feel good about yourself, because that may be one of the few things that you have control over for the time being.

Critical Questions:

- What is your budget for maternity wardrobe purchases?
- Are you comfortable with some of the budget-friendly options offered, or will you be shopping retail for all new items?
- What are the must-have wardrobe items required to be presentable in your industry?

Real Simple:
Strategies to Avoid Overwhelm

If you aren't overwhelmed yet, you might soon be. At some point in the pregnancy, it hits you that you might not have any idea what you are doing, what to expect, or really how to prepare. If you are successful in your profession, it might have been a while since you last felt this clueless and overwhelmed. Just like you do in your chosen field, start by learning the basics and remember that any problem can be solved in bits. As the saying goes, even an elephant can be eaten one bite at a time. So let's look at ways to keep things simple, from the things you need to buy to the things you need to do.

Buy Buy Baby

There are more baby websites, stores, and products than you ever thought possible before you joined this club. Here's one sure way to avoid being overwhelmed. *Don't buy anything just yet.* Get all the information you can, whether by talking with friends, researching online, or reading the latest books and magazines. There is a wealth of information out there, and once you get into the groove, you are likely to be able to figure out what makes sense for you, your lifestyle, your business, and your family.

One of the most amazing social customs I know of is the baby shower. Having gotten married later in life, I had absolutely no use for a wedding shower, which would have added too much stuff to our two-household dilemma. But when it came to baby stuff, I didn't know where to start. Amazingly, the baby shower solved ninety percent of my procurement problems. You might also score a mini-shower called a "sprinkle" for a second baby. While I admit that I dread getting invited to showers (mostly because of the silly games and bad punch), it was just amazing how friends were willing to share in our little one's arrival.

It is fine to drop hints to a best friend or family member that you are interested in a shower, and you might want to register at a baby store just to let your parents know what would be useful gifts. But be careful that you not even hint or put pressure on employees or (God forbid) clients to host or attend such galas. If it's meant to be, they will offer.

If you have the good fortune of receiving baby items from friends and family as they hand off their gently used baby items, don't immediately turn them down. Often friends are trying to make room in their own place, and they are happy to see items go to a good home, sometimes temporarily and sometimes permanently. Say yes to their generosity, and later you can selectively replace items. By making the most of this kind of generosity, you might think outside the big box store for gifts you really want that won't be on the registry. The gifts you might need the most will help you save time so you can still attend to your business and your family, like these below:

- Meals- You might be lucky enough to be part of a community, neighborhood or family that offers up a casserole caravan. Whether you are a foodie or vegan, these meals can be a godsend. I welcomed them for what they really are: a thinly-veiled reason for friends to drop by and see a precious newborn. In almost every culture, shared food is the ultimate expression of caring. If others offer to cook for you, don't dismiss them, as self-sufficient women have a tendency to do. Say yes, and enjoy the few days you can spend with your new family without having to deal with food details.

- Cleaning- If you don't have a cleaning service, you might be able to ask friends to help you with the tasks of keeping your home together. It may feel strange to hand your vacuum over to others, or have an organized cousin clear out your fridge, but these are blessings of a full heart. Welcome them and enjoy your baby. If someone gives you hired cleaning services, even better.

- Organizing- Not everyone can have a professional organizer visit or needs to, but if you are overwhelmed with space, gifts, and gear, a professional can help you feel in control in just a few hours. If you are still working, it might be a very wise investment, more than paid for by the revenue that you could otherwise be earning in your business. Setting up the nursery or clearing off the dining room table might be just the thing to make you feel sane. If you have a generous friend who has this talent, set up the parameters that you feel comfortable with, and let her help you.

- Diapers- They aren't sexy, but they are necessary. If you are using disposable diapers, you will need an unending supply. Many people don't like to give them for a shower gift because they are not the type of gift that will be kept and cherished forever, but you can put the word out that you are looking for a sizeable stash. Estimates are that you will spend about $2,000 on disposable diapers until potty training. If you are using cloth diapers, the very good quality versions and the accessories (quality soap, diaper pail liners, wet bags, and cloth wipes) are still pretty pricey (but relatively less than disposables at about $600 for an adequate stash of high-end cloth diapers). I used both disposables and cloth diapers with both of my girls. Today's cloth diapers resemble high-performance systems and are very easy to use if you have a washer and dryer on site. Gift givers might be very interested in kicking in for your cloth diaper supplies, especially if they are eco-conscious.

- Massage treatments- I could spend time here justifying this one, but really, any mom will back me up that you are going to need a few minutes of R & R sometime after that gorgeous little bundle arrives. If you have a few massage gift certificates stashed away, they can feel like get out of jail cards for the days when you need a little treat.

Resale, consignment, swaps, freecycle.org, other online sites offer you another great resource to avoid getting overwhelmed. If you aren't plugged into the baby sub-culture, chances are you might not know what is useful, trendy, consumable, and durable. Online reviews can help you decide what to do and what to get. It became clear early on that I didn't need to purchase any toys for my tot...ever. Between the gifts that the grandparents could not be talked out of getting, and the finds on swap sites and at thrift shops, I could stock a whole toy room inside of a week for next to nothing. Since we don't actually have a toy room, having this information cut down on the random toys that would become clutter in our home. By reading up on recommended toys and products, I was able to get some really great items for almost nothing just by keeping my radar up or as gifts for special holidays.

Are you overwhelmed yet with all the changes you will have to make in your house? How can this tiny body require so much stuff? It seems like there is at least one huge baby item (playpen, high chair, crib, swing, bouncer, jumper, playpen, and more) added to each room of your home. If you are making changes to your space, like converting a guest room into the nursery, you may not know how things fit together until you actually start making the changes. There is a process you can follow to break it down. Start with the big pieces, like the crib. Purchase and assemble this piece first, since it is the only one you must have. Yes, you can have your little one in a bassinet for a number of weeks and maybe months, but you're going to want to get some sleep before long, and the crib is the place where the baby will go, or no one will be getting enough sleep. Even if you are in a small house or apartment, plan on having the baby's space set up before the baby comes. If you wait until after the stork visits, you'll be juggling everything you are already juggling, plus a little warm body who needs someplace safe to sleep. Be sure to set the crib up in the room it will actually occupy, since it won't fit through doorways once assembled. Once you have the crib figured out, re-use, repurpose, and redesign your space using things you already have. Don't rush out to buy baby furniture if you already have pieces you like. A functional dresser you already own that is sturdy and your style can be a budget saver. With a changing pad on top, you might have the perfect changing table already on hand, without having to deal with delivery men and making room for more furniture.

Whenever you are tempted to accept or purchase something, ask yourself, "Where will I store it?" This goes for the big and the small items. If you've lived in your home a while, chances are you've decorated and filled it with stuff already, so some things might have to leave to make space for your little one. This is a chance to get organized and feel more in control of your space. Don't even think about stashing your excess in the closets because you'll need those for the baby's stuff, too. The baby will have regular bedroom closet items, along with baby towels in the linen closet, baby coats in the hall closet, baby blankets in the storage space, and baby toys in the basement. Use what you have first, and creatively redesign the baby's closet so that it can be reconfigured in a couple of years, when the baby's clothes change out for toddler's clothes and then teenager's clothes.

If this doesn't sound like fun to you, call a decorator, professional organizer, or closet professional right away. Of all the things you must accomplish in your business before this baby arrives, this may be an easy way to get things accomplished without having to use your valuable brain cells or time slots.

A Room of Her Own

If you work from home, chances are you have converted a bedroom into your office. If you are really unlucky, you've been running your office from a corner of the living room, the dining room table, or maybe even a tiny little slice of your own bedroom. Does the baby now get your office? You still need a space, even though the baby is going to take up the nursery, the playpen is going to occupy the corner of the living room, the high chair is going to be the new fixture in the dining room, and a new rocking chair for nursing will be situated in your already full bedroom. You get the idea. Little ones come with a lot of stuff. But if you are going to continue to operate from home, you still need a designated space, perhaps now more than ever. One option you might have is to convert a closet into a private office space. If you can clear out a standard reach-in closet, you can customize it with a desktop and enough shelves to hold all your computer gear, administrative paperwork, and product samples. To make it super functional as a multi-tasking space, simply ensure that the doors close and add a rolling chair that goes with the décor of the room. A custom closet company can customize a six to twelve foot closet for about as much as you might pay for a medium-quality desk. If you go this route, be sure to have an electrician add outlets and lighting. This might end up being your favorite space in the house once you decorate it to your taste.

Figure 1: This home office was customized from a standard reach-in closet. The shelving on the left was designed to hold the printer and electronics. The desk was customized with a shallow book shelf below and a shallow pencil shelf above. A professional electrician added electric and internet connections. Attractive storage boxes keep collections and clutter contained. The entire closet can be converted back to a closet for hanging clothes with a few simple changes. The formerly hard-to-reach space behind the right door was re-built to provide shelving outside the closet that is accessible from the room and provides even more storage.

If you must share a workspace space, a room-dividing screen might provide you some separation. However, be sure that the screen is secure, perhaps mounted to the wall or securely wedged between two larger pieces of furniture. Otherwise, it will become a hazard for your new baby in about six months when he or she starts crawling and walking.

If neither of those options work for you, consider purchasing what I call an office-in-a-box. You can find this type of clever armoire, designed to hold computers and office gear, in many home furnishings stores and online. They are a substantial piece of furniture, but they look more attractive than a cluttered desk. They also allow you to close the doors at the end of your work session, so you don't have to see or be bothered by work items. They can often be repurposed down the road for household storage.

Figure 2: This type of office-in-a-box solution, or office armoire, can close completely to allow you to leave your office behind closed doors when needed. This image shows the Cantata office armoire, courtesy of Riverside Furniture. [35]

Case Study

Gretchen started a business a few years ago creating and distributing artfully-crafted guided-question keepsake journals. Like most businesses, hers was created out of a personal need and market void. Her business was small but established, with nationwide distribution in a boutique retailer. At the time of her third pregnancy, her biggest business problem was where to locate her office. The baby was awarded the former guest room/home office, her desk moved to the basement, and her inventory moved to the attic. With relatively small space needs, this rearranging didn't present a major change in her business, but did allow her to creatively redecorate the shared TV/playroom, which now also housed her home office.

Go out if you must. If you have completely run out of room for your home-based operations, it might be time to investigate rented space. Work with realtors in your area or network with your colleagues to find appropriate space where you can run your operations. The major downside to this, besides additional cost, is that you won't be able to work at odd hours in your pajamas. However, if you need a presentable space that allows you to visit with clients, separate space might be an absolute necessity. If you need only occasional space, and can still stand to store all your administrative work at home, then look into executive office suites, often available by the day or the hour. There are many reputable firms that operate nationwide, and you might have a local provider in your area:

- Regus.com
- HQ.com
- ExecutiveCommons.com
- AmericanExecutiveCenters.com

Many, many businesses have been started at kitchen tables and in garages. But once Junior enters the picture, I really encourage you to stop using the kitchen table. Many women are trying to run a small business from the space underneath their bed, their nightstand, their dining room, or even a dedicated space in their basement that they hate. Mentally legitimize your business so you can feel comfortable rearranging your family's space to support your business. Whether you move a desk into your own bedroom, convert a closet into a home office, or just clear the junk out of the guest room, make that leap. You can carry on a hobby from anywhere, but you need your own space to run a business. Your own space gives you credibility, even if credibility starts with just yourself and your spouse. It sounds much more professional to tell clients, "I'll send that to you when I return to the office," rather than, "...when I return home." A separate space also means that your business supplies, some of which may not be child-safe, are going to be secured and available when you need them. Having your own supplies and computer are a must. Can you really take a chance that Junior might damage your customer database by pouring juice on it? Allowing kids and your business to occupy the same space is a recipe for chaos. No matter how cute it looks, don't let the baby chew on your cell phone. Those hardworking items are the lifeblood of your company's communications department. Several hundred dollars after making this mistake, I put the baby gate up on the office door and instructed everyone at home not to let our baby chew on any cell phones, lest she get a hold of mine again.

Organize for Your Sanity

There seems to be two kinds of people. Some women seemed organized before they had kids, but after kids declared themselves a hopeless mess. These women probably didn't have organizing systems, but only simpler lives before kids. On the other hand, women who established some structure and systems before they had kids tend to stay organized as they add to their families. This is, of course, a little bit of an oversimplification, but there is no doubt that women who are more structured even for a small family have a better shot of keeping track of more complexity. Even if your business is completely creative in nature and you crave the creative process, there is no denying that having some routines and systems helps you be more successful.

I have worked with many women who operate product-based businesses, including sales reps and managers for toy distributors, Mary Kay, Arbonne, Longaberger, Tupperware, and the list goes on. In these types of businesses, product is often all over the place. You need to have a space to store and a space to pack your orders. You also need a separate place for materials for parties and shows, with display materials, banners, and order forms ready to go on a moment's notice, like in an egg crate or a rolling bag. Sounds basic, but it's not always obvious. Most of these franchises offer plenty of paper to keep track of leads, orders, payments, and parties, so setting up the paperwork isn't a problem. But making all the paperwork accessible so you can complete your paperwork (in the ten minutes a day you have for it) and keep great records is the key. A dedicated space is a must. Blank forms can be organized in horizontal stacking trays (of the in-box style) or a form-sorter. You can usually stack the paper in trays in the order it gets used. Trays allow you to see when you are getting low on, or overloaded with, a particular type of company form.

The written word is powerful, especially when it comes to the calendar. Whether you prefer paper or touch screen, keyboard or stylus, writing something down is more likely to make it happen. This is absolutely true when it comes to scheduling. If you don't already keep a calendar, start now. You have a few months to get in the groove. Moms are famous for keeping a kitchen wall calendar, but you need something that travels with you during your day. Keep just one calendar, which operates for both personal and business commitments.

You only have twenty-four hours in a day, after all, regardless of whether you are using those hours for personal or business appointments. If other people make demands on you, ensure you can see those commitments in real time, or near real time, so that you can avoid overbooking yourself. It's best if you are able to view a whole month at a time, since daily views of your calendar keep you in fire drill mode. How can you be strategic if you only ever plan for one day at a time? Have monthly page views available for the next year. Make sure you have calendar views all the way through your planned maternity leave, since you will almost certainly have personal and business commitments during your stated leave period. Business owners never truly get to take time off, after all.

As for scheduling your actual calendar, here's a little time management tip that can take you from frazzled to fabulous. Start scheduling your personal time into your business calendar. Whether electronic or personal, most people tend to use calendars to fill up white space with commitments to other people. So, if there is a blank space on next Wednesday's page, you rush to fill it with a client. Sometimes other people who are not clients are also filling up those slots, such as family members, home maintenance vendors or business associates.

Usually the personal stuff, even the important stuff, gets pushed and pushed until there is no time left on the calendar. This is how people become stressed, with a sense that there is no time to eat right, exercise, or tackle the big strategic projects in their own lives. Business planning, organizing, self-care and networking can fall into the *important but not urgent* category that never gets scheduled and completed.

You have my permission to start scheduling yourself into your own calendar's white space. So if you need to take a nap during your pregnancy, schedule it. Code it creatively if other people actually see your calendar. You could record something like: Mtg w/Simmons. If your exercise program never seems to get off the ground, start writing in every Thursday night for yoga, and stick to it. Allow yourself time for commuting to and from your personal appointments. Doctor appointments need to be scheduled as often as once a week towards the end of your pregnancy. If others are able to see your calendar, you may want to code-name these appointments if it seems unprofessional to you to list them as your OB/GYN appointment on a shared calendar. Sadly, even time for grocery shopping and nutritious meal planning can evaporate if you aren't vigilant. If you are constantly left hitting the drive-thru after appointments because there isn't time to visit the grocery store, then perhaps you can start thinking of the grocery trip as a procurement trip, or a mini-outing with your newest staff member. Whatever the case, write it down on your calendar, and it is more likely to happen.

It often takes three to six weeks to get a new ongoing activity scheduled into my calendar. The upcoming couple of weeks are always already booked, so I try to schedule in meetings and new commitments starting next month or even the month after. If they occur on a regular basis, I schedule them in for the remainder of the year and avoid conflicts because I can plan ahead and request alternative times to meet colleagues and clients.

Remember that usually when people are asking for your calendar time, they aren't particularly interested in why you may not be available. Start censoring your responses, instead of saying, "I'd love to, but I'm meeting with my obstetrician then." A simple, "I'm not available then. What other time would work for you?" will do. Especially when you are talking with professional colleagues, clients, or prospects, they don't need to know the details of your personal life. They don't need to know that you are going to your prenatal yoga class, just as they won't need to know that you are having babysitter issues in a few months. Follow the tried and true KISS principle, and Keep It Simple Sweetheart. A straightforward, "I already have an appointment then. Can we try another time?" is all that's needed.

What you really need, though, are realistic goals for the

sleep deprived. The sleep deprivation might start well before your delivery date, but it only gets worse for most of us after the big day. Although you may be the master of the universe on an ordinary day, you'll be completely normal if you have many pregnant days (mostly in the first and third trimester) when you can barely accomplish your daily makeup routine. It helps to know that after delivery, success might be measured in accomplishing just one major task a day, and that task might be emptying the dishwasher. Your mileage may vary, but a set of realistic goals and a good calendar can be your friends that allow you to be the healthy incubator that you need to be right now.

There are list people, and there are people who abhor lists. Even if you are in the list-hater camp, you need lists for your mommy brain. We've already established that mommy brain is a real thing. According to Donnica Moore, MD, a women's health expert based in Far Hills, New Jersey, pregnancy brain "should serve as your first tip-off that when you are preparing to have a baby, you need to simplify other areas of your life, because life is about to get a lot more complicated."[36] As the victim of an unfortunate combination of circumstances: sleep deprivation, a hectic lifestyle, heightened hormones affecting brain function, and more things than usual to track and care for, what you need are survival strategies. The number one strategy for dealing with mommy brain (besides getting as much sleep as you can) is to write things down and keep lists for planned activities.

The real value in lists may simply be that they allow us to stay focused. I have a particular strategy for keeping a to-do list. Instead of a daily list, I recommend keeping a weekly list, and ensuring that it covers both work and personal commitments. The Pareto Principle, otherwise known as the 80/20 Rule, outlines that about eighty percent of the important stuff in life comes from about twenty percent of our activities. On a dated page of your planner, draw a line about twenty percent of the way down the page. Things that are "must do's" get written above the line (pay taxes, make doctor appointment, return a client call, etc.) The things that are nice to do, or perhaps longer term, get written below the line. This strategy instantly prioritizes your life. The list only gets rewritten once a week, saving you time and giving you more flexibility than a daily list; you don't need to sweat that you didn't get a particular task done on a certain day. The brilliant thing about this system for mompreneurs on the go is that you only have to decide if the task at hand is a random thought that will need your attention sometime later, or if it is a critically important task that should absolutely be attended to this week, which goes above the line. You can see an example of how this works in the appendix C.

The benefit of having lists is undisputed and well documented. David Allen's book, *Getting Things Done*, boils it down to keeping a list with you everywhere so that you can do a constant data dump, and your thoughts become actionable instead of scattered.[37] By allowing your brain to quit processing the same item over and over (creating worry, anxiety, missed deadlines, and unpleasant consequences), you free up mental energy. In *The Checklist Manifesto*, Atul Guwande quantifies the outcomes of codifying routine events, like pre-surgery preparation and pre-flight aircraft checklists. If a simple 12-step checklist deployed by the World Health Organization can significantly reduce the amount of infection from surgeries worldwide,[38] then a simple checklist to help ensure that you have everything you need to leave the house for a client appointment, for example, can't hurt.

While your thoughts require checklists, your stuff needs routines. Put your keys on a hook when you come in the door. Place your cell phone on a charger every time. Park in the same spot at the mall. Assign a home for all your household items. Clear out your kitchen sink every day. Make sure that incoming, unopened mail has a safe place to land inside your front door that doesn't mix with other papers. Have a place in your office for your computer bag where you won't trip on it.

None of these routines are astounding, but they are essential to save your sanity, and perhaps make your home safer. If you are not already doing them, start now, before your baby comes. Communicate with your spouse and see if he can get on board with improving the routines for your jointly owned stuff. You might be surprised with how much he enjoys the changes. If you explain that you are trying to improve how the house works so that you'll have more time to enjoy as a family, he just might be all over it.

With your thoughts and your stuff organized, that only leaves paperwork. Unfortunately, paper is the modern bogeyman for many adults. It isn't going away, and by adding more people to your life, even tiny ones, you'll be adding more paper. Don't drown in business or new baby paperwork. If you ask a business owner why they went into business, they usually say things like, "So I could work with my hands," or, "Because I love my particular product." They almost never say, "So I could do my own paperwork."

In business, you need to be able to access information when you or your customers need it. If you've struggled in the past with organization, chances are this is something you'll struggle with as a business owner until you get a plan together and systems in place that work with you. Of the information that crosses your desk, you might not know what is valuable right away. It is helpful to think of your business information as three different types, and physically divide your office and even your computer into these types of spaces:

1. Active
2. Reference
3. Archive

Before we look at these three types of information, let's quickly examine your real estate. Do you have a designated place to *run your business*? Where do you put your business paperwork before you get a chance to work on it and after you complete it? Do you have a clear space where you can work on a project? Do you have designated spaces to hold important information that you need to reference daily? Do you know what is in any given pile of paper on or near your desk? When you sit down to run your business, how do you know what to do next?

Instead of getting overwhelmed, realize that a successful business owner makes time and space to both *do the business* (the fun part) and *run the business* (the paperwork part). Since you are also probably the executive of your household, you'll need a place to do that, too. When you run the business so that customers get what they need, bills are paid on time, and you are making regular deposits to a healthy bank account, then the *running the business* part of your day or week becomes the fun part, too. I'm not kidding.

Let's go back to the three types of information and decide what they are and how to store them. First, let's look at the Active information, which is anything that earns you money or directly affects your ability to earn money. Active information requires clear and immediate action or is referenced frequently. Unfortunately, it can be devilish to organize because it can be on post-it notes, business cards, or other random paper. Some of these things may also be stored in a mobile device or gadget. Examples might be:

- Sales leads
- Accounts receivables (payments you get to deposit)
- Active client files
- Your calendar
- Bills to pay
- Your checkbook
- Your passwords
- Your contacts (address book, online contacts, rolodex)
- Product and inventory orders to vendors

- Upcoming business travel arrangements
- Current projects, such as planning an event
- Current commitments, such as those for a professional association
- Forms used on a daily basis
- Reports completed regularly, as in franchise reports

The Active information is the type of paperwork that you use daily, several times a day, or weekly at a minimum. Only this type of information should be anywhere near the flat surface of your desk. In fact, this information should usually be on top of your desk so it is in your view, or at the very least within reach without leaving your chair. If you aren't sure what your Active papers are, sometimes it helps to write down what your process flow looks like. With a process flow, even a simple one, you can usually see things like leads and paid orders shouldn't be anywhere near each other, or that leads are getting thrown in a drawer, never to surface again. Simple paper systems can be implemented, like an index card box or a monthly follow up file sitting upright in a repurposed wicker basket. If you have access to electronic customer management systems like Outlook or ACT, great, but you need to know how to use them, otherwise just use paper forms. Technology is great, but only if you use it.

The top of your desk is very valuable real estate. Think of it as the penthouse real estate. You don't want to clutter your most valuable asset. When you sit down to run the business, you want to have everything at your fingertips to be able to make money, and not have distractions lined up in front of you, whether they are paper clutter or a line of princess figurines. If you have things on your desk that aren't Active, they probably fall into the next category.

Reference material is anything you've already looked at that is valuable to keep (not just a nice to have), but you are only referencing between once a month to once a year. These things should be labeled and filed away, perhaps in temporary storage boxes or in a sturdy file cabinet. Ideally, the reference material would be located in the same room as your desk, whether you work at home or in a rented office. Reference material is still valuable and should be kept orderly so you can find important documents when needed without losing time that you could be spending on the Active information (income producing) above. Types of reference material include:

- Past customer files (individuals, venues, or organizations)
- Insurance policies (business liability, medical, other)
- Your company website plans and history
- Current year tax records
- Sales tax registration
- Business licenses
- Trade name registration
- Employee records
- Advertising plans
- Custom printing orders
- Warranties and manuals for business equipment
- Software disks, product registration and keys
- Items you have written (newsletters, articles, template letters)
- Accolades file for letters of appreciation or reference letters from clients
- Professional association memberships
- Your resume (Yes, you should have one, even if you work for yourself.)
- Business plan
- Budget
- Marketing plan
- Reading list
- Business idea file

- Vendor agreements
- Product information and catalogs
- Reading material (articles, books, product information)
- Forms that aren't used frequently

Archive materials, the third category, are the equivalent of rented storage units of your real estate metaphor. In fact, they might quite literally be in off-site storage. These materials do not need to be in your office because they are usually referenced less than once per year. These should still be at least somewhat organized, usually in filing boxes or cabinets. They should be labeled with content, year, and in most cases, the length of retention (or date of destruction) according to your business data retention policy. (If you don't have one of these, you can research your own guidelines on the internet or hire a professional organizer to help you develop one.) Just a note of caution, business records should never be stored in a household basement, garage, or attic if at all possible, since those areas are particularly prone to damage from water and critters. Your business records have real financial value, so you'll want to protect them in the same environment you live in or in secure off-site storage. Since archive items are referenced infrequently, you don't want to have these on your desktop, and you don't want them where other employees or family members might mistake them for worthless pages. Some types of archive materials might be:

- Business startup or incorporation papers
- Previous year tax records, including paid bills
- Mortgage, rent or loan documents
- Business automobile records
- Bank and credit card statements
- Training and Certifications obtained, certificates and/ or manuals

- Past closed legal matters
- Off site storage inventory
- Past completed projects, such as construction records or past events

Your business will undoubtedly have other types of information than those listed here. Decide what type of information it is (Active, Reference, or Archive) and store it appropriately before it overwhelms your desk. After all, you went into business to do what you love and make money, not dread your desk. After a short period of setting up your office with these three types of information and real estate zones to support them, you can *run your business* more effectively leaving you more time and energy to *do your business* and produce more income.

The last type of paperwork that you will have is baby stuff. Whatever you do, separate the baby stuff from your business stuff, even if (especially if) you really do run your business from your kitchen table. Good systems now will be invaluable as this type of paper starts to grow. This happens in just three short years, which is when Junior starts preschool. Right off the bat you'll have three types of baby paper and information:

- Medical
- Vital records
- Memories

The medical documents related to your pregnancy are likely to be short-term paper. Assuming a healthy pregnancy, you'll be able to shred much of your doctor bills, hospital handbook, and what-to-pack checklists after all the bills have been paid by your insurance provider. If you or the baby develop medical complications, you'll want to keep more of the documentation for at least a short period, and maybe longer.

The vital records include the birth certificate, the Social

Security card, and the immunization records. More may show up, including savings bonds or bank account records, college 529 plans, and medical histories if your baby has any special medical conditions.

The memories start now, including the sonogram and computer images of your little one in utero (which are memories, not medical), the foot prints made at the hospital, the first pictures, the shower invitation, the cards accompanying baby gifts, and all the rest that comes along with your little one. I recommend getting a memory box now and dropping memory items into it so they don't get lost or mangled. When you have some quiet time, in about six years, you can start your scrapbook, if that's your thing.

Lastly are the photos. Chances are your photos will be mostly digital. It helps to have a naming convention for photo file names so that you'll be able to find them again later. Your computer file system will want to arrange your files either alphabetically or numerically. After trial and error, I arrived at the following naming convention for my files, which keeps my files neat and allows me to find files quickly:

Format: Year_Month_Kidname_Event/Holiday

Example: 2010_April_Kylie_Easter

Just knowing that you have several types of paper and information to organize might help you reduce the overwhelm factor that is likely to creep up on you in these last few months before delivery or immediately after. Try to divide and conquer so that you can spend time where it is really important, with the people in your life.

Critical Questions:

- What is overwhelming you right now?
- If you could get any kind of support right now, what do you think would make your life easier? How can you make it happen?
- Where will you work once the baby arrives?
- What changes do you need to make to ensure your workspace is conducive to working?
- Does paper, time management, or physical clutter stress you out? Which strategies outlined above could help you the most?

CHAPTER
9

Disclosure:
Who, When, and How

Some things you want to shout from the mountains tops. Maybe you've spent a very, very long time waiting to hear the doctor say those magic words, "You're pregnant." You probably want to tell everyone. But wait.

Just like most things in your business, disclosing your happy news may require a strategy. First, consider your partner. He's the first one who gets to know, so take some time to think about this. How will you tell him? How can you create a fun memory that both of you will cherish for a long time? This isn't just one more thing on your to-do list. This is BIG. This is a wonderful secret the two of you get to keep, at least for a while. You've probably both been busy lately; this might be a very different kind of news in your lives. If it is hoped for, expected news, how can you make it fun? When I was sharing the news the first time, after a particularly grueling weekend course, I stopped to purchase a baseball mitt and a copy of *What to Expect When You Are Expecting*. My head was pounding from a killer headache, but I couldn't wait to see the look of bewilderment on his face when he opened an unexpected gift. I explained that he was going to need the baseball mitt for little league. He thought I had volunteered him as a neighborhood coach until he saw the *What to Expect* book underneath. Simple, but it was a precious memory, and we carried on a completely different kind of dinner conversation that night. For the second unveiling, I had purchased two pairs of teeny-tiny baby shoes (the baby version of blue high top sneakers and pink ballet slippers). During dinner this time, I mentioned to him that I needed his advice on two pairs of shoes I had purchased that day. It only took him a few seconds to catch on, but it was a fun little game for my husband, who loves scenarios. Remember, the time between when you find out you are pregnant and when you want to or need to tell him could be very short, so have some fun with it, but make it snappy.

Here are some ways to tell your husband you are pregnant:

Pooch Delivery

I wrote "Mama's Pregnant" on a piece of paper and attached it to our dog's collar. When my husband came home, our dog ran to greet him. Once he realized what was going on, he couldn't stop beaming.

Colleen, San Diego, California

Made with Love

One night, when my husband came home from work, I told him there was something sweet in the oven. When he opened it up, he found a large bun on a plate. Puzzled, he just stood there until I shouted, "Honey, there's a bun in our oven!" He was so shocked, he didn't believe me.

Melissa, Alexandria, Virginia

Spell It Out

My husband and I are huge fans of Scrabble. So, when it came time to tell him we were expecting our first child, I couldn't think of a better way to share the news than to spell it out while playing our favorite board game. My husband was ecstatic!

Sally, Destin, Florida

Shirting the Subject

Once I discovered I was pregnant, I embroidered a shirt for our 1-year-old son that read, "I'm a Big Brother." I put the shirt on our son right before my husband came home from work. He walked in, read the shirt, and became very excited.

Tricia, San Francisco, California

A Sweet Surprise

I planned a theme dinner for my husband. I made baby corn and carrots, baby back ribs, and for dessert I walked out with a big red bow around my belly, holding a small bowl of Sugar Babies. He loved it!

Carla, Allentown, Pennsylvania

Seeing Red

Minutes before my husband came home, I wrote "You're a Daddy!" on my belly with bright red lipstick. The look on his face was priceless!

Rachel, Camden, Michigan

The Secret's in the Sauce

I created a label that read "Andie & Michael Are Prego" and placed it on a jar of pasta sauce. That night, I suggested we make spaghetti for dinner. After handing my husband the jar, I watched him carefully. Within seconds, he was grinning from ear to ear!

Andean, Olney, Maryland

It's in the Bag

My husband is a golf addict. When I found out I was pregnant with our first child, I gave him a gift bag. Inside was a onesie that said "Daddy's Future Caddy." He was so happy he cried.

Judith, Hazlet, New Jersey

On the Bottle

I made dinner plans at our favorite restaurant and dropped off a baby bottle that I had decorated and written "It's a Baby!" on beforehand. That night when we arrived for dinner, I asked the manager to serve my husband's beverage in the bottle. At first, my hubby was totally baffled, but once he read the bottle's message, he quickly leapt out of his chair with excitement!

Heidi, Kailua, Hawaii
Originally published in American Baby *magazine, May 2005.*[39]

To tell our parents we are going to get baby frames and on a blank card put a stamp of baby footprints in black ink. Above the prints will be written: We are extending our home by two feet. Below the prints will be written: Additions to be completed in (month baby is due).[40]

I'll empty his sock drawer and fill it with newborn diapers, a Buffalo Sabers onesie (which I already bought!) and a note saying "Make room daddy... I'm moving in!" I have a feeling he'll get a kick out of it since we're always saying how we're going to have to really make room.[41]

If the pregnancy is a surprise to either you or him, remember that men and women deal with life's news differently. Hopefully you are in a loving, supportive relationship, but this is not always the case. He may be concerned about your business and ability to continue to work and earn a living. Men also, and I hate to generalize here, do tend to see this new baby as an additional financial responsibility. If your guy fires back at you on this level after you share the news, just realize that his whole gender is wired to do this. It is still true in our culture that men nurture through their wallet. His response may or may not have anything to do with his actual concerns and his level of commitment to either you or the baby. This is where it is good to remember that men are from Mars, as the saying goes. He may need some time and space to digest the news and be able to strategize with you about it. If you've already had some time, even just forty-eight hours longer than he has, recognize that he may need his own forty-eight hours to level out and be the responsive, thrilled daddy-to-be that you want him to be.

Once he is in on the secret, agree with your spouse on whether or not you will be sharing the news right away with others. Some folks just can't keep a secret, and that's fine, too. Conventional wisdom says to keep the secret through a comfort period of the first three months. Whether this is your style or not is completely up to you.

One reason to delay putting the news out on the social media wire is to give yourself some breathing room before you get everyone's opinions. Opinions are like belly buttons, everyone has one, and they are happy to share, whether you've asked for it or not. They may have opinions related to your partner, your age, your housing, your work, or just about anything else you can dream up an opinion on. That doesn't mean you'll hear them all, but if you don't want to hear any, keep the news to yourself until you have some sense of how your affairs might be affected in the coming year.

Family

It has been said that happiness is having a large, loving, close-knit family…in another state. There are basically two kinds of family, those who live near you and those who don't. OK, that's boiling a very complex situation down past simplicity, but whether your family is long distance versus local may affect how and when you unveil your news. We chose to tell no one at all until we were twelve weeks along.

At twelve weeks, since I was carrying the baby, I got to tell my mom first. I thought that was fair, after all. I asked my parents to keep it under wraps, which was next to impossible.

I just had to be OK with the fact that my out-of-state family would do what families do, and that is pass information along the grapevine. In your case, take some time to agree with your partner who gets told first, next, and so on.

Telling your family can be almost as fun as telling your spouse. For my long-distance parents, we mailed them a package and told them not to open it until they called us. When they saw the book we sent, Dr Seuss', *Oh, Baby, the Places You'll Go: A Book to Be Read in Utero*,[42] they immediately started laughing. We slipped an ultrasound image in with a bunch of recent photos that we were sharing with his mom, just to throw her off the trail. If you aren't expecting it, it's surprising how strange a black and white sonogram looks.

Regardless of whether you live near your large, loving, close-knit family, or whether they are in another state, they are entitled to hear your news before you tell the groups that we will talk about in the following sections. Your family is likely to be the most interested in your news, period. They are also likely a great source of support in many, many different ways. Don't let the rumor mill do your job when it comes to staying in touch with important family members.

Clients

Clients are in a whole different category. Depending on your past client interactions, the type of services you provide, and the amount of contact you have with your clients, you might run the gamut from a strictly professional reaction to a very personal (sometimes too much so) interest in your situation. As long as you are still wearing your old jeans, you need not feel any responsibility to tell them anything, but once you start busting out the maternity duds, they are going to ask questions. This will happen sometime between month three and five, or maybe earlier if you are tossing your cookies every day. Questions they ask will cover anything from the obvious ("Can I ask you something? Are you pregnant?") to the more oblique ("Do you think you'll be able to lift that?").

Your clients might assume that you'll be staying home, not working at all, or cutting back to a part-time enterprise once the baby comes. People will, largely based on their own experiences, have expectations about your availability and ability to serve their needs. Unless you specify what your services will be post-baby, you leave it up to their imagination, which may not reflect positively on you. Don't leave it to chance; communicate your business goals. At eight months pregnant, I took steps to solidify commitments into the next year by booking clients and speaking engagements, and by starting a Board of Advisors for my small business.

You'll want to have a story and a strategy ready before you ever tell your news, especially if your clients depend heavily on you. And when you think of it, which of your clients doesn't depend on you? Clients will be wondering:

- What if you can't do the same work?
- Will you be able to finish their project?
- When exactly will you stop doing the things you've always done?
- Do you have an assistant to take over?
- Will you be subbing out work for a time?
- Will you be answering your phone during your leave?

During my first pregnancy, I decided to wait quite a while before I shared the news with my clients because I didn't really know how long before maternity leave started. I didn't know whether I would work right up until I delivered, or if I would have to stop doing my client work well before that. It turns out that I did complete physical work right up until my delivery date in both cases. I did have to tell a colleague in confidence that I couldn't assist her because there was a possibility of hazardous materials on site. Someone overheard the conversation or she shared it with someone else she thought needed to know. I was never quite sure what happened, but soon random people knew my news. It wasn't a big deal, but it was clear that I wasn't as much in control of the information as I thought I had been.

In another situation, I shared with a client in March that I would not be handling installations beyond June, in an attempt to allow her enough time to make a decision and place an order. In sharing that information, I knew I was opening myself up to the possibility of early disclosure, but I wanted to be open and also ensure that I could meet her timeframe. She ended up scheduling the job just before I took my leave.

Public speaking is also part of my business, and I sometimes book engagements up to a year in advance. If your situation is similar, decide now if you will be able to follow through. If you have an engagement that is close to your due date, even a month or two prior to your due date, situations beyond your control could prevent you from upholding your commitment. Of course, if this happens, most reasonable people will be completely understanding. Having a backup plan for this period in your life is just a good idea, and your host is likely to think more of you if you have been up front with them. Your backup plan may include rescheduling, offering to run a teleconference instead of an on-site event, or having a colleague step in if you are unable to deliver, so to speak.

You might be concerned, but disclosing your status to clients can be done professionally. I was contacted by a new client in my ninth month to organize a law office. After the phone interview, I determined that I could take the job two weeks before my due date, but I had to prepare him for a very pregnant woman meeting him on the job site. I joked with the client that, being a professional organizer, I was fully intending on delivering on my due date (which I did), but that if I were to unexpectedly go into labor before then, I might not have time to call and cancel the appointment. He was a wonderful client to work with, and we accomplished what we needed to in advance of my delivery. I also was able to squeeze in several installations the week before my due date, at client requests. Through clear communication, I was able to schedule these appointments and keep cash flow positive right up until my due date.

Employees & Contractors

If you have employees, they'll need to hear the news from you at some point. Don't make the mistake of assuming that close employees are just like family. Their agenda is not yours, and your news may make them nervous. They may immediately wonder about your commitment to the business and your intention to keep it running so they can keep collecting a paycheck. All kinds of scenarios could play out based on your business, your relationship, and your history with your employees. If you work closely with sub-contractors, while not exactly the same as employees, they may have an expectation about your relationship, and it is a good idea to communicate with them as well.

If you have been struggling with your business model, this change in circumstances may be a great thing for you and your employees. Can you develop key employees quickly? You might be able to give them added responsibilities that would allow you to do less in the short-term and do more strategic things in the long-term. Do you need more focus on account generation or key client development? Perhaps you can train a member of your staff to do more operational tasks, like running deposits or routine follow up with past clients. Be prepared to be surprised with your staff's abilities. People usually relish the thought of taking on more responsibility.

Good communication facilitates success. Communicate your plans and expectations for changes before they occur. Don't expect individuals to run the store while you are out if they have not been prepared. You may feel like you have a full plate, but part of the job of an employer is to manage employees. Be ready to share a plan for how they will work while you are on leave. Have a discussion with them about what would happen in the event of your medical issues suddenly cropping up before your due date. Consider getting help for jobs you might not have needed staff on before, such as installations or bookkeeping. These might be actual or virtual staff.

This is a great time to stop doing things you don't like, especially if you can delegate them to your employees. For instance, I managed a great deal of my website and my business technology myself up to a point. Although I could keep doing that during off-hours, I needed those off-hours back to draft customer proposals that I had been handling during available client time. Since techie stuff was not my strength, I pushed more of the technical projects off to contractors and vendors who could accomplish that service faster and with better quality. This is almost always a good strategy, especially when you have a real deadline to beat and only so many hours in the day. Use this strategy with anything that you dread or dislike doing, especially if it is not the core of your business.

This might also be the time to think clearly about the division between doing the business and running the business. If you have always done the technical aspect of your business, (like doing the plumbing in the plumbing business, or the accounting in the accounting business), you might be in a good place now to test how shifting the technical work completely to your technicians will improve your operations. If you don't already have employees or technicians doing this, there may be adequate time to find and train these technicians to carry on in your absence, but it will depend on your business.

Case Study

Whitney opened a brand-new retail shop for fine women's accessories in September. Within the month, she realized that her sluggishness was due to her new baby bundle, not the workload associated with opening a new store. She and her husband decided to share the news only with family for the first three months. Early on, they told Whitney's sister and fellow shopkeeper, who was not a great keeper of secrets. Whitney's sister was so proud that as soon as she was allowed, she was bursting to tell everyone, including the UPS man, about Whitney's happy news. Whitney was grateful that her second trimester, the highest energy period of her pregnancy, arrived just in time to get her through the Christmas retail season, while she worked on getting key staff in place, ready to operate without her if needed. Once the cat was out of the bag, her happy news helped Whitney to build rapport with her mostly female clientele and make many new friends during the first months of her store's existence.

Everyone Else

Walt Disney got it right with the ditty, "It's a small world after all." Once you tell your spouse, your family, your clients, and your employees, there will still be people left to inform. You may start to feel like everyone knows, but that won't be true. There will be colleagues you haven't seen in a while who might need catching up. There might be those polite enough not to make assumptions, even though you feel as big as a house. It just isn't socially savvy to assume someone is pregnant if you aren't sure. What if you were just gaining weight without being pregnant? It does happen.

Just remember, you don't control the information flow now, if indeed you ever did. Social media and social networks have increased the speed of personal information tremendously. Even if you aren't Facebooking constantly, chances are that someone in your universe is. My rule of thumb on important news, whether it's, "We're pregnant," or something more somber, is to share the information in person or on the telephone whenever possible. Emails and posts are a very impersonal way to share anything, despite the fact that the younger crowd is always connected. However, things are changing fast, and not everyone agrees with me. Sometimes email is the most efficient way to get the word out.

While many people are going to be happy for you, business colleagues and clients are never as concerned about you as they are about getting their own problems solved and needs met. This isn't a bad thing, it's just reality. Commerce is about meeting needs and expectations. Once you've shared your news, if necessary, move the conversation and focus back to the client. After all, they are presumably still paying you to solve their problem or meet their needs. If you are not able to do that because of your pregnancy, then be honest and straightforward, just as you would want someone to be with you. Don't be known as the woman who shares too much information (TMI). Not everyone cares as much as you do right now about healthy eating, weird skin issues, various body fluids, and how much sleep you are getting or not getting. Keep it simple and professional, no matter with whom you are talking and no matter what size your business is. Your reputation will only improve.

Critical Questions:

- How do you plan to share the good news with your partner?
- Do you and your spouse agree on the plan for telling others?
- When will you share the news with each group listed here?
- What concerns do you think your clients and customers might have once you reveal your news?
- If you have employees or subcontractors, what can you do to ease their transition through your pregnancy and maternity period?
- Is there a key employee that you could bring on or develop to take on tasks while you are away?

Build Your Team

Most people who work for someone else dream of autonomy. Maybe you want to stay home or to work nearer to home to spend more time with your baby. Maybe you'd like to have the freedom to set your own schedule. Maybe you've had one micro-managing boss too many, and you would just like to take a turn at being the boss for once. Maybe you have a thousand ideas of how to provide a better customer experience. Maybe you'd like to keep more of the profit. Maybe you want the choice of when to work overtime and when not to work so hard. Maybe you have exhausted all of your local employment options and no one is hiring, and if you are going to make money using your talents, you must start your own firm. These are among the many reasons that we go into business for ourselves.

Many business owners want a shot at going it alone. However, successful small business owners know without a doubt that they can only succeed by working with others. If you came from a corporate setting, as I did, you'll quickly find that the first few months of researching and actually being in business can be frightening, and perhaps lonely, simply because you don't have the staff and structure that you were used to. It sounds great to make all the choices for your business, but when you are struggling with something that is not your area of expertise, you come to respect the support that a larger company can give you. You may get intimidated, scared, frustrated, or stymied in your decision making. All of this is understandable, but by no means a show stopper.

In this chapter we'll discuss your team, even if you are a single-person business. You probably already have some team members working with you. It's time now to identify them and identify where you have gaps in your team so you can round out your support. We'll explore how to find your team and how to communicate with them during the next few months. Finally, we'll talk about one of the most important team members you'll have over the next few years, your childcare provider. Even if you have a teeny-tiny business and you want to stay that way, knowing that you have a team can be a very liberating idea.

Let's say you've had a small business for a few years, and you've decided that you want your business to stay relatively small. That's great. That decision alone might be something you want to write down and refer to, maybe in your strategic planning document that is for your eyes only. Of course, you can also decide that you want to grow or change your business to a more sustainable model, or you want to lay the groundwork for some big changes to your business over the next few years. You can also be working with a business coach to develop your business in specific ways in the future. Your business could go in any direction, so it is essential to have a general strategy written down so that you can continue working towards your goals without getting easily thrown off track.

Staffing

The traditional model of a store or other operation running with employees may be just the thing for you. However, we have more options today than ever before. You may have a storefront that requires actual people to be there to open up and turn the lights off at the end of the day. These actual people may be employees. More and more operations today, however, are using a mix of contractors, virtual operations, and outsourced staff to ensure that the day to day operations get executed.

If you choose to bring on contractors, be aware that the Internal Revenue Service (IRS) outlines conditions under which a worker can be legally classified as a contractor versus an employee. The IRS provides some guidance on this topic at www.IRS.gov by searching employee versus contractor. The IRS uses three characteristics to determine the relationship between business and workers: behavioral control, financial control, and type of relationship. There are several guides at www.IRS.gov that are helpful, including IRS Publication 15-A, Employer's Supplemental Tax Guide; Publication 1779, Independent Contractor or Employee; and Publication 1976, Do You Qualify for Relief under Section 530?; Form SS-8; and Form 1099.[43] Just like employees, contractors can come with their own challenges, such as turnover, motivations that are out of sync with yours, and inadequate training or skills. Contractors can also be a great fit to add specific skills to your operations or allow you to have enough people-power to respond to a given opportunity. Given the timeframe that you have before your due date, consider whether contractor labor is a good fit for you.

If you are determined that the operation will continue without you at the helm, consider outsourcing. You may be able to find skilled, even expert, resources that can continue some or all of your activities from a remote location. Often the infrastructure required will be a professional website, a well crafted job description, automation tools such as email auto-responders, and perhaps logistics support such as packing and shipping facilities. Today you can find all of these resources via sites on the internet. You can outsource almost anything from web development and accounting functions to writing, organizing, design work, phone response, even sales and client management. Document a clear written expectation of the support you are requesting, and have a clear understanding of any agreement that you enter into with an outsourcer.

Whatever you do, keep an eye on Return on Investment (ROI). Sometimes you need CPA to assist you with ROI calculation. However, you can usually calculate it yourself. For instance, when I decided to outsource my bookkeeping, although I was able to do it myself and it only took about five hours a month, it was a really easy decision. When I hired my provider, she converted my books to QuickBooks, which allowed me better management of my finances and better clarity at tax time. My bookkeeper could do in two hours what took me five hours. I was happy to pay her an hourly fee when I could be out making double that or even more. Even after a few extra hours that it took to set things up initially, the ROI payback period was about a month, and I was able to be back out earning money while my bookkeeper was working for me.

Identifying Your Team

If you really are a smaller business, like thousands that have one owner/employee working out of a home office, you need another approach. Let's stop and take inventory of those who can help you. You may be an expert, but you can't do it all. How are you going to find support staff for the things you can't or don't know how to do? Do you need to hire someone to do everything? In a word, no. This is the magic of true networking. Offer to share your knowledge on a professional level with others, and they will do the same for you.

I'll give you an example. When I started my business, the idea of hiring a lawyer and a CPA was terrifying to me. I thought CPAs and lawyers had more letters behind their names because they were smarter than me, and I couldn't afford them. I sheepishly called a friend of mine who I had heard was a CPA. I apologized for taking up her time, and asked if she knew of an accountant who handled small businesses. Really small businesses. Actually, I called my business *small potatoes* during that call. It took me weeks to make this call, I was so intimidated. To my surprise, she responded right away that her entire business was made up of really small business clients, and she would be happy to meet with me in her office to figure out what I needed. No charge. Yippee!! I was thrilled. She took a look at my simple spreadsheet that I had been running to keep track of my income and expenses. She advised me to keep doing what I was doing. She explained a few deductions that I wasn't aware of. Then she explained what information she would need to file my taxes and how she would charge to do my taxes that year. She provided so much valuable information that she saved me much more than the couple of hundred dollars that I would eventually pay her to prepare my taxes at the end of the year.

Something similar happened with my attorney. One day I got a call from my attorney who had recently prepared our wills. I had mentioned to him that I was thinking of starting my own business, and he called to see if I would be interested in joining his networking group. I did, which worked out wonderfully, since he was happy to answer my basic, quick questions in the first few years of business during breakfast, again without charging me. It previously never dawned on me that many lawyers and CPAs are self-employed small business people, too, and they also need to stay connected to their market to win new clients. In the few instances that I have needed specific legal advice, I have felt very comfortable calling him because I know his fee structure, and I know that he is honest because I've worked with him in the past. When I do pay for his expertise now, it is a justifiable, deductible business expense that I know I can afford.

When I worked in the corporate world, I had a legal staff and an accounting staff supporting my department. Today, it's just me, but by doing some low-key networking, I am not left operating my business without these two very critical support pieces. My bookkeeper, who I met through a mom's group that I belong to, does a great job for me every month. We mail information back and forth, and I never meet with her except for social occasions.

One mistake new small business owners make is expecting

reciprocity in networking. There should be no expectation that your support partners are also developing business for you. In my experience, a business relationship is almost never equal. I often share my painter's name with clients, because that is a service that many of my clients need. I am happy to share his name because he does good work on time at a fair price. However, I don't stop referring him to clients just because I don't receive the same number of referrals from him. If I can offer good recommendations to my clients, then it benefits me because they see me as a knowledgeable source for other resources, and they are likely to contact me for other things. This is just one more way that networking benefits you; it goes way beyond generating leads.

Take a moment to list all of your support staff for your business in the chart below, even those who are not employed by you. In addition to those basic business functions listed below, you might have other trusted vendors specific to your business. For instance I consider my painter and my electrician as part of my support team, since they often work with me on design jobs. Think who you work with regularly and include them in this list. Include team members on both sides of the business:

Doing the business (technical mastery)
Running the business (administration)

On the following page, use the form (also found in appendix D) to list out your staff and partners for both sides of the business.

Your Company's
Super Simple Staffing Support Plan©

Function	Contact
Bookkeeping	
Board of Advisors	
Branded promotional items	
Certified professional accounting	
Childcare	
Childcare backup	
Contractors	
Employees and managers	
Graphic design	
Human resources and benefits	
Insurance	
Legal	
Marketing	
Photography	
Printing	
Service providers (e.g. painter, electrician)	
Suppliers, product vendors	
Technical/computer support	
Videography	

Virtual assistance	
Web design	

It is very common to run a small business without a formally recognized support team. But you are about to go through a time when having a network that is really talented and committed to you is going to be very helpful. Take a moment to call them, send an email, or write a note and enclose a couple of your business cards. You don't need to sell anything. Just let them know that they are appreciated. Think how you would feel if you received a note of appreciation today from someone you respected. You might say something like:

> "Dear Vicky,
>
> I just wanted to thank you for being my attorney. Your excellent advice has helped me be a better business owner over the last five years. I wish you continued success in your own business.
>
> Fondly, Darla"

If sending a handwritten note, be sure to include two business cards. One is for them to keep, and one is for them to share with a potential client.

Networking

Do you have names in all of the slots on the chart above? If not, this is where professional and informal networking is valuable. No, I don't mean those insufferable luncheons where you pay for bad food and forced conversation. And I also don't mean social media exclusively. While you may choose to do some of that, those bits and bites alone don't always develop real networks. Take a close look at your memberships and meeting commitments. If you are super involved in your local Chamber of Commerce, and you can positively quantify the number of leads and revenue or valued resources that you are developing from that experience, then it is probably worth continuing. There are many great networking options, including Christian Chambers of Commerce, Le Tip, and Business Network International (BNI) networking groups.

Personally, the second I found out I was pregnant, I dropped my membership in my local lead networking group. Although it was a great group of people, I had quantified that the two years of dues I had invested had barely been recovered by business from referrals, and I knew that I could not attend breakfast meetings through the exhaustion of pregnancy, and certainly not through the sleep-deprived months of infancy. You may have a completely different experience, but right here, I am giving you permission to exit any networking group that doesn't fit into your schedule or plan. This, by the way, is called being strategic.

On the other hand, there may be groups that you have wanted to explore. After I left my lead group and freed up two hours a week, I had enough time on my calendar to visit with a Christian networking group that met for lunch only twice a month. I was able to attend a couple of lunches and see what they were about. I was thrilled to meet a completely different set of professionals, and find out that the structure of the group was much more my style. I decided not to formally join, but I am still on their mailing list, have attended their events, and contacted members when they offered a service that I needed. I went from attending a group whose focus was lead generation to associating with a group that offered vendors that I could add to my support team. Since I was in the process of slimming down my client hours, I didn't spend so much time spinning my wheels on lead generation for other companies, which was a requirement of my former group. I now had several other area resources that I could call when I needed to advance my business.

Consider your time commitments when exploring networking options. Up until now, before kids that is, you've been able to set your own schedule. During pregnancy, you may still be able to attend almost anything you can scribble into your electronic calendar, but you may decide that you need to schedule a little more personal time. Think ahead at least a year, and decide if the group's meeting time will be something that is likely to work for you. If you are planning, like I did, to be home for your kids during the day most of the time, then perhaps the best groups for you to connect with are those who meet during the evening if your husband can watch the baby. Choose groups who meet less often, or who don't have a stringent attendance policy.

Getting involved is the best way to benefit from groups where you belong. If you are involved in formal networking groups already, you probably know this. You may decide that you want to join in a committee to stay plugged in or help execute a certain event that the group offers. But if you haven't already announced your big news, only take on those commitments that you know you can fulfill before your delivery date. Volunteer committee work can have very high visibility in your network, and you want to be seen as someone who can deliver on your commitments, rather than someone who isn't reliable.

Networking can be done on a budget. If you have a business or if you are just starting out, you probably know that joining formal groups can be pricey, costing hundreds of dollars a year in many cases. Building your team through networking doesn't have to suck up your entire annual marketing budget.

- Visit the group as a guest. Many groups offer visitors the chance to attend for free or a nominal fee for one or two visits before they ask you to join. Take advantage of this, and be sure to get contact information of those you'd like to stay in touch with. Just because you decide not to join the group doesn't mean that you can't keep in touch with that great shop owner you met at breakfast.

- Learn more about the groups that you already are involved with. Do you belong to a church or synagogue? Do you practically live at your local library? Is there a volunteer fire company in town? Do you attend a country club or a local golf event each year? Are you passionate about some cause, like cancer research, pet shelters, or the League of Women Voters? Find out how to volunteer for these organizations. Chances are you'll spend about the same amount of time on networking, but you'll be able to meet an entirely different group of folks than you would normally run into at your town's dominant business networking groups. I find that this is such an interesting way to meet all types of people, and referrals from people who come to know and respect me through these groups are the biggest part of my business.

- Offer to speak to groups. If you love your topic, chances are you could tell people about it for hours. If you've never spoken before, create a short talk entitled, "Top 10 Mistakes People Make with (Your Topic)," and offer to give that presentation for free at local community groups. Remember that public speaking is one of the top universal fears, and only people who are knowledgeable and passionate can pull it off; you fit both of those categories. People will come to regard you as an expert and will either contact you for advice or referrals over time.

- Call or write to all of the vendors that you have used personally over the past couple of years. Did you have your kitchen remodeled? Call the contractor and let him know what kind of business you have. You want to do two things: offer information and offer a way to stay in touch. You aren't selling, just getting the word out. So a simple phone call might go like this:

"Hi Rob. This is Darla. You remodeled my kitchen last year. We still love the great job you did on the tile. I am still bragging about you to my friends. I am calling to just mention to you that I have just opened a karate studio in town. Next time you are downtown, why don't you stop in and see what we're up to? We'll be offering kids and adult classes. I am so excited about it, and parents tell me that their kids just can't wait to get to classes. To thank you for helping us out last year, I'm going to send you two passes for a free class. You can use them or pass them on to your friends or clients. I hope I'll see you soon."

Note that you can have this conversation in real time or with someone's voice mail. Remember to follow up with your offer, and always include two brochures or business cards in any mailing you send out. One is for your contact to keep, and one is for them to pass along to others. If you have a customer list, also mention to the person that you will be adding them to your email list, always giving them the option to opt out. This approach is simple and doesn't cost any more than a one minute phone call and a stamp.

- Join your industry's professional organization. Almost all industries have their own association. Search the internet and find the group that provides educational opportunities for you. Even if your association does not meet locally, chances are there will be opportunities to meet at a national conference or regional events. Networking at a professional association of peers may not get you leads, but it will help you stay current on trends, learn about the hot topics facing your type of business, and will improve your credibility. Networking in these associations may, indeed, offer client opportunities. If your colleagues either can't provide a client service in your geography or specialty, they may send clients to you. This happens all the time. In fact, I send potential clients to my colleagues every single month for a variety of reasons. If you have the opportunity to do this, you build good will with clients and your peers.

Board of Advisors

One more part of your team may be a Board of Advisors. Have you heard of a Board of Directors? Certain corporations and other organizations, perhaps even yours, operate with the benefit of a Board of Directors. These are formal positions. This Board serves many functions, but at its simplest, it is a group of people to ensure that the company strategy is appropriate and in line with long-term goals. Who will provide you strategic oversight and sound professional advice to your small company? A Board of Advisors consists of people you choose who advise you on strategy; however, they do not have the fiduciary and legal obligations that a corporate Board of Directors would have.

You can develop your own Board of Advisors. Establishing a Board of Advisors now signals your intention to strengthen your business, improve your professionalism, and continue operations after your pregnancy. It is a precious chance to learn from other talented people, all willing to help you succeed. Perhaps the best benefit is that you create a formal accountability to your Board that you might have never had before. Just the act of having to explain your strategy and your business activities to someone else, and provide periodic updates to them, is a powerful way to keep you focused on your goals. Boards also have a way of periodically stopping and making you celebrate your accomplishments, since no one else is likely to do it for you.

There is a method to determining who should be on your Board. Start by determining what your strengths are and where you need assistance. If, for instance, you are an expert on marketing but you are not a numbers gal, then perhaps you need to bring in someone who excels at financial analysis and strategy. The people that you might ask to sit on your board should be professionals, not simply friends, who can add some specific perspective that you want to strengthen. Consider your mentors, successful business owners who may be in completely different lines of business, and experts in a particular field. Board members need not be located in your city, if you are comfortable convening conference calls. Diversity is a good thing to strive for. A number of college friends in the same business discipline, for instance, might not make the best Board of Advisors. Your spouse does not get an automatic seat on your Board. You only need enough Board members to provide you with a well-rounded picture of your strategy, most likely between three and five advisors. Approach each of them with a well thought out request. What type of time commitment will you ask of each of them? What type of prep will they be asked to complete? Explain why you thought to ask them, and what particular skill you think they can offer to the Board. For many people, being asked to assist you in this way will be a compliment, but don't be surprised if one of your chosen candidates says that they can't fulfill your request. Paying members of a Board of Advisors is not necessary, but you should let them know whether you will or won't compensate them when you make the request for their time.

Once your selected candidates agree to be on your Board of

Advisors, communicate your goals and your major challenges. Share your work/life balance issues. A good Board will assume that the operations level of your business is something you know how to do well, but they will offer support on the major challenges that you are facing, and they will provide their unique perspective for you to consider. Carefully listen to their advice, even if you decide to implement it in your own way. Communicate with regularity, even if you only meet with your Board by teleconference a couple of times a year. Keep them up to date on your operations throughout the year so they can help you when needed. See appendix E for a template of a monthly or quarterly update for your Board members. Remember that while your Board members are sharing their expertise and brain power with you, you might have a chance to mentor or assist other business owners in a pay-it-forward fashion.

If you choose not to have a Board of Advisors, that is fine, too. Most small businesses have never considered or heard of this idea. Not everyone needs a Board or will be comfortable with one.

Childcare Options

One of the most important players on your team is your childcare provider. If your childcare provider is a solid member of your business support team, then you'll be able to better focus on your business. If this part of your team is not solid, then running your business will be a real challenge. There are plenty of good options to explore.

- Family members
- Institutional daycare
- Home-based daycare
- Mom & me classes, story time, camps
- Baby swaps
- College students

- Live-in or part-time nannies
- Au pairs
- Spouse
- You

Numerous resources can help you through the details of what childcare options are open to you based on your location, your budget, and your needs. Childcare is one piece of your business puzzle, not an afterthought. Look for the flexibility or structure that you need. Research and network as many options as possible. If you make one decision and it doesn't work out, you can change it. Just like your business, you may have a few false starts before you find the right childcare solution. Rest assured, when you think you have it all figured out, your situation may change yet again.

My situation was challenging because I underestimated the amount of time that I would need to work on the business. I admit it, this was a blind spot. I knew I didn't need and couldn't afford full-time daycare. I spent a year feeling like I was constantly looking for someone to watch my daughter for just an hour or two. In her second year, I put the word out among friends that I was looking for someone who was willing to come to my home just one day a week. When we hired our regular sitter, I was relieved that I didn't have to worry about who was watching after my daughter, where she was going, or what she was eating. She got to nap in her own bed, and our sitter respected any special instructions that I left. I felt like I had cloned myself for a couple of hours each week. I could meet with clients without having to worry about my daughter in the back of my mind. If I ran late with a client or ran into traffic, it was never a problem with my sitter. When baby number two came along, I didn't have to change those arrangements at all. I offered her flexibility, too, since my sitter could choose which day she wanted to work, according to her class schedule, and she could change the regular day with a month's notice.

Some women with flexible schedules and variable incomes have a chicken and egg issue with childcare. Should you hire the childcare first so you can ensure the possibility of income, or should you schedule the jobs first and hope you can find childcare when you need it? My advice is to schedule the childcare first and schedule the jobs into your allotted time. After all, your kids come first. While it may seem costly the first day you have your childcare paid for and no paying clients scheduled, you can always use more quiet time to accomplish tasks at work. Use this time to run the business, if you have no client work. Also, remember to include the price of your childcare in your business costs and prices. If necessary, raise your prices. Yes, it's unfair that your colleagues without children don't have this cost in their business, but there's no use crying about it. Every business is unique in some way. Your colleagues may have been through this stage already, and you will be on the other side of it someday, too. Start planning to pay a sitter as soon as your defined leave period ends, and maybe even before.

Once you figure out the childcare solution, consider what your backup plan is. Sitters have car trouble. Kids get sick. Schedules change. Things happen. You are likely to need more than one childcare solution this year. Take a moment to think about what the solution might be for you. Could family help out occasionally? Is your partner able to spot you when disaster strikes your schedule? Are there drop-in daycare centers in your town, and have you checked them out?

Case Study

Michele is an art dealer who has offices on both coasts and travels for her business. Her primary office is in her home. Her husband is also self-employed, but works outside the home. His mother is a nanny who was looking for a new position about the time that Michele became pregnant. The perfect solution was to ask Michele's mother-in-law to move in with them for the first three months after the baby arrived. With a separate guest suite, their house allowed them the luxury of on-site childcare and relative privacy. Their plan is to find a local nanny or daycare center so grandma can move back to her permanent home. However, for the short-term, this arrangement seems like a great solution for everyone.

If you need flexibility from your childcare provider, ask for it. In-home childcare providers, family members, and part-time nannies may offer this level of flexibility. If your spouse has a flex schedule at work, or if he is also self-employed, he might schedule a day off for a period of time to let you continue your workload. However, you become like two ships passing with one of you always with the children and the other out working. If you have this arrangement, make a special effort to connect with your spouse as a family or as a couple, because it is too easy to fall into a routine that doesn't foster your relationship. Schedule date night and special family time, even if it is just once a month.

Baby swaps sound like they should be illegal, but it is just another creative way to get the help you need. This arrangement can work out well, especially if you just need a few hours each week. Find a friend or colleague who is willing to swap babysitting time. For example, you would agree to keep her kids each Tuesday and she would agree to keep yours each Wednesday. Communication and flexibility are the hallmarks of good baby swap arrangements. Just beware, because having one new mom in charge of two babies might be a little overwhelming. You might look for a friend who loves babies who now has a preschooler at home. Like any childcare situation, realize that there might be environmental challenges. Does she own a huge dog that you worry about? Do you own a cat and your friend is allergic? Test it out before you need to be away for hours for a big client meeting.

Hopefully you've considered who is on your team, who you might need to recruit to your team, where you might find them, and how to engage the right childcare solution for your needs. Now let's go make some money.

Critical Questions:

- Who are your support partners or team members in your business?

- Which support partners are you missing, and how can you fill those gaps?

- What networking commitments do you need to add, change, or remove from your current schedule before the baby arrives?

- Can your business continue to operate while you are away? Are there employees or subcontractors who can carry on while you are out? Have they been able to operate without your presence before? Will your clients accept this from you?

- Is your business seasonal or time-sensitive? Will you be absent from the business during a peak activity season? Can you prepare your clients in some way for this absence?

- Would it benefit you to add a Board of Advisors to your business?

- What childcare provider solutions make the most sense for you, and how will you test them out?

- What is your backup childcare solution?

CHAPTER
11

Show Me the Money

There might be plenty of reasons that you are in your chosen business, but there is only one reason to be in business, and that is to make money. This chapter will help ensure that your business is financially successful.

Wouldn't it be nice if you got paid for your maternity leave? The Family and Medical Leave Act of 1993 (FMLA), administered and enforced by the US Department of Labor, entitles workers to take up to twelve weeks of unpaid, job protected leave every twelve months for specific family and medical reasons. Not only does FMLA probably not apply to you, it only provides unpaid leave. It only applies in certain situations. First, it is offered by employers, so if your firm is Me & Me Alone, LLC, FMLA will not provide you anything. Even if your company is large enough to be an employer, and you are one of the employees of your corporation, the corporation must have at least fifty employees. And finally there is the requirement for twelve consecutive months of employment, adding up to at least 1,250 hours of employment during those twelve months. So if you were hoping for some relief from the federal or the state government as a small business, sorry, but you are out of luck here in America. This chapter is about preparing your finances and creating a financial plan that allows for you to customize your maternity leave. This is too important to wing it. Grab a calculator and let's run those numbers.

There are as many types and forms of business as there are individuals, so some of this may or may not apply to your situation. It's time to evaluate whether your business is a viable business. Viable means profitable. Really profitable, not just kinda-sorta-maybe. This means we need to do a business review and some planning.

Let's start at the beginning. You are in business to make money. This needs to be said because women often start businesses for reasons other than money. For instance, you may love your field. You may be an expert, in fact. You may have started a business to support someone else's dream, such as your spouse or friend. You may have inherited a business from your parents. You may have entered into your own business to fill your time. Or you may consider your work to be your spiritual mission. All of those things are laudable, but the common denominator is that your business must be profitable or it can not exist for long.

There is nothing wrong with money. You might have heard that money is the root of all evil. This is actually a misquote from the Bible, which says, in 1 Timothy 6:10, "The love of money is the root of all evil..." Money is simply a tool within our society. Having or earning more or less of it does not make you a better or worse person. Dave Ramsey quips that when you do a good job, your clients give you certificates of appreciation; those certificates of appreciation just happen to be called dollars and are backed by the full faith and guarantee of the United States Treasury.[44]

PLEASE DON'T SKIP THIS CHAPTER. Don't worry, you don't have to have an advanced degree in business to do this. You have put thought, effort, and energy into your business. You are doing the same for your lovely new baby. This particular planning step can help you decide, with laser-focus, how you are going to get the time you desperately desire to get ready for your baby, and how you are going to be able to enjoy more initial time with him or her.

Remember the Super Simple Business Plan© you started filling out in Chapter 2? Keep it handy as you go through the next few exercises. You may decide to change some of your goals and inputs.

Paying Expenses While on Leave

If you already have a financial business plan for your business, compare your assumptions on the next few pages against your recent results, and revise your plans accordingly. Follow the steps below if this is something you've never done before.

First, figure out what expenses you'll continue to have in your business while on maternity leave. The template below will help you get started, and provides examples of expenses that continued in my business during my four months of maternity leave. Replace these expense items and figures with those that apply in your business. Both fixed expenses, which occur whether you are operating or not, and variable expenses, which occur in greater or lesser amounts according to your operations, should be included. A blank copy of this form can be found in appendix F.

Your Company's
Maternity Leave Expenses Projection Tool
Period Covering Projected Maternity Leave: months/year

Date	Payment Type	Vendor Name	Memo/Description	Amount
9/15/2008	Check	WebHMG	website development	$0
10/15/2008	Check	EZ pass	auto	$100
11/15/2008	Credit	Professional Association 1	dues	$260
9/10/2008	Credit	Professional Association 2	dues	$125
8/9/2008	Credit	Professional Association 3	dues	$250
9/9/2008	Credit	Professional Association 4	dues	$175
10/19/2008	Check	Liability Insurance	insurance	$147
12/31/2008	Check	Liability Insurance	insurance	$157
9/25/2008	Credit	ConstantContact	newsletter	$30
10/25/2008	Credit	ConstantContact	newsletter	$30
11/25/2008	Credit	ConstantContact	newsletter	$30
12/18/2008	Credit	ConstantContact	newsletter	$30
9/15/2008	Check	Bookkeeping ABC	bookkeeper	$50
10/16/2008	Check	Bookkeeping ABC	bookkeeper	$50
11/12/2008	Check	Bookkeeping ABC	bookkeeper	$50
12/3/2008	Check	Bookkeeping ABC	bookkeeper	$60
11/8/2008	Credit	lunch w/CPA for year end planning	accountant meeting	$50
10/10/2008	Check	State sales tax	sales tax due	$199
12/1/2008	Check	newspaper	subscription	$25
12/1/2008	Credit	Radio ad renewal	annual marketing	$60
12/13/2008	Check	GiftsRUS	Holiday gifts for customers	$120
9/16/2008	Credit	USPS	postage for holiday gifts	$40
11/24/2008	Check	ICS	computer support	$200
		Total Expenses		**$2,239**

Salary- Owners Equity @$600/mo   + $1,800
Best Case Expenses for Total Leave Period $4,039

Let's now move to your personal living expenses, which have almost nothing to do with your business plan. How much do you personally need to get paid? This question usually gets blank stares when I ask it of business owners, but this question is the right starting point. How much salary do you need? The first question that drives pricing strategy isn't how much money can I make or how much can I charge, but how much salary do I need to make this business worth my time? As a business owner, your salary is either a corporate expense or, in the case of a sole proprietorship and partnership, a non-deductible expense. Either way, you need enough profit to clear your business expenses and still have some left over for you. So how much money do you want to have each week, month, or year? Fill this number in on the worksheet on appendix G on page 210.

Some readers skipped this step thinking that they don't really need a salary, since their spouses pay all the bills. Some people are in business for years and never take a salary from earnings. Some people are just not sure that there is enough profit in the business to take a salary. Congratulate yourself on covering your expenses, but then think about what you are worth. Yes, you deserve a salary. Even a fast food restaurant employee could clear at least $240/week take home pay on a $10/hour wage in a forty hour work week. Are you able to take that much out of your business for you to spend as you please? Even if you think you don't need a salary, even if your salary will be spent on manicures and massages, decide what your salary should be. If this business is the family's sole income, and you haven't yet answered this question, the answer is even that much more critical. Read on.

Business profit is simply your revenue (income) minus your expenses (bills).

Revenue – Expenses = Profit

Your personal expenses (your salary) are only part of the profit figure. If you are to grow your business over time, you'll want to build in enough profit to invest in periodic expenses like new training, economic challenges, expanded capacity, and labor/outsourcing. To review, revenue minus expenses equals profit. Profit equals your salary plus a cushion to grow.

Profit = Your Salary + Investment in the Business

A simple example follows:

You decide you need $200/week for personal bills & expenses.

You have 10 hours a week that you can work in your small business.

You determine that you can make $100/hour, or $1,000 per week. That's your revenue.

Your business expenses are $600 per week.

Revenue- Expenses= Profits

$1,000 - $600= $400

So far, so good.

You determine that to pay for anticipated growth and training, you need to save (or invest) $50/week. This must come out of your profits.

Profits= Your Salary + Investment in the Business
$400= $200 +$50 +X

If you noticed that the last formula didn't add up, congratulations. In this example, X equals $150 a week that could be added to your business savings account to pay for future expenses and growth, or could be paid as additional salary to you, the owner. In the situation that you are in, pregnant, that is, that extra little bit of unallocated profit becomes very important to your planning.

Let's look at a model situation. Follow along on the example here, and then fill in your own worksheet in the following section. Let's say that you find out in January that you are pregnant, and your small business is currently earning roughly $1,000 per week with the above expenses, profit, and salary requirements. Let's also assume that you are having a routine pregnancy that allows you to continue to work in your business. And let's say you decide that you want to take a full three months away from the business when the baby comes, and that no income will be generated while you are not working in the business. There are other ways to plan for this time and ensure that income does continue, but let's look at this situation for now. Finally, let's assume that you are not the only breadwinner at home, and that your spouse will be able to keep his income and expenses steady during this time. Now let's convert weekly to monthly figures. The first chart shows what the business looked like before you got pregnant. Notice the positive salary and unallocated profit, otherwise known as savings, and existing reserves:

Super Simple Pregnancy Profit & Loss Snapshot ©	Pre-pregnancy monthly figures
Monthly Revenues	$4,000
(minus) Monthly Expenses-fixed	400
(minus) Monthly Expenses-variable	2,000
(equals) Monthly Gross Profit	1,600
(minus) Required Salary	800
(equals) Monthly Unallocated Profit (savings) or Loss	$800
Reserves (amount in your business checking account)	$7,000 existing

During your pregnancy, things change slightly. Perhaps you don't have as much energy, or perhaps you are spending time on more strategic, long-term activities. Your revenues might dip a little, but the business is still profitable:

Super Simple Pregnancy Profit & Loss Snapshot ©	Pre-pregnancy monthly figures	Pregnancy (January- July)
Monthly Revenues	$4,000	$3,200
(minus) Monthly Expenses-fixed	400	400
(minus) Monthly Expenses-variable	2,000	2,000
(equals) Monthly Gross Profit	1,600	800
(minus) Required Salary	800	800
(equals) Monthly Unallocated Profit (savings) or Loss	$800	$0
Reserves (amount in your business checking account)	$7,000 existing	$7,000 existing

You decide to take three months off from the business completely, and here's where your reserves will carry you. While you are not working for three months that you've planned to take off after the baby arrives, fixed expenses such as insurance, internet access, and service contracts that you have in place still need to be covered. You may still have some variable expenses, but they are likely to be lower than if you were working.

Then, determine whether your salary requirements will change at all. For instance, if part of your salary goes to pay for gas and lunches out while working, you may be able to cut back on expenses during those three months. You'll probably still need some income, but you may be able to reduce it, say from $800 to $600/month. On the flip side, you probably won't want to hole up in your house for three months. Do you need an increase in budget to pay for cute new baby gear and a daily latte at the corner coffee shop? Whatever your answer, evaluate and plan your course.

During the three months you are taking off in our example, you can decide not to or may not be able to save for growth and training in your business. You may also not have any unallocated profit, otherwise known as savings. In fact, it is likely that in this case you'll be drawing from your reserves, or living off of your business savings. By drawing down your reserves by $1,000 each month, you reduce your business reserves to $4,000. See how this looks in the example below:

Super Simple Pregnancy Profit & Loss Snapshot ©	Pre-pregnancy monthly figures	Pregnancy (January- July)	Maternity leave period (3 months, Aug-Oct)
Monthly Revenues	$4,000	$3,200	0
(minus) Monthly Expenses-fixed	400	400	400
(minus) Monthly Expenses-variable	2,000	2,000	0
(equals) Monthly Gross Profit	1,600	800	-400
(minus) Required Salary	800	800	600
(equals) Monthly Unallocated Profit (savings) or Loss	$800	$0	-$1,000
Reserves (amount in your business checking account)	$7,000 existing	$7,000 existing	$4,000 remaining

Finally, post maternity leave, you begin to ramp up your revenues again; however, this takes time. Your revenues aren't what they were, but since this is a lifestyle business, you are making a conscious decision to spend more time at home with your new baby:

Super Simple Pregnancy Profit & Loss Snapshot ©	Pre-pregnancy monthly figures	Pregnancy (January- July)	Maternity leave period (3 months, Aug-Oct)	Post-baby ramp-up period (9 months, Nov-July)
Monthly Revenues	$4,000	$3,200	0	$2,000
(minus) Monthly Expenses-fixed	400	400	400	400
(minus) Monthly Expenses-variable	2,000	2,000	0	1,000
(equals) Monthly Gross Profit	1,600	800	-400	600
(minus) Required Salary	800	800	600	800
(equals) Monthly Unallocated Profit (savings) or Loss	$800	$0	-$1,000	-$200
Reserves (amount in your business checking account)	$7,000 existing	$7,000 existing	$4,000 remaining	$2,200 remaining

By planning ahead and managing income levels and expenses, your reserves in your checking account financed your leave period. No one gets rich in this example, but it shows how you can actually take time off and return to a healthy modified re-entry schedule. What type of schedule and workload do you want to have upon completion of your leave? Do you want to head back into your pre-baby schedule? Do you want that first full year as a part-time buffer period? If so, this may impact your earning ability. I intentionally ramped down my appointments for the first year after each of my daughters were born. I felt very fortunate to avoid negotiations with an HR department and not wonder if I'd have a job when I returned. I simply scheduled only the clients that made me happy. I only accepted jobs for a few months that were within a reasonable commute, meaning that they would fit within my three hour nursing schedule. Flexibility like this is priceless.

Every mommy magazine that you've ever read probably has an article that states some women decide to stay home from their previous employment because the cost of commuting, keeping a professional wardrobe, and daycare expenses eclipse their take home pay. In your self-employed business, you decide what your take home pay is. Figure out how much money it will take for you to leave your baby and go to work, or to hire the kind of childcare that you really want for your child.

After maternity leave, I experimented with outsourcing some business functions and bringing on additional help for key jobs. I still needed to work, both for the income and to get a break from endless diaper days at home. I was able to keep my skills sharp. I continued earning, although not as much as I had previously.

A funny thing happened. I started to choose only my target clients who resulted in more profitable business. This business principle makes so much sense when you hear it, but is hard to translate into your own business until circumstances require you to start making hard choices. When my maternity leave ended, I sometimes had to decide whether I'd rather take a relatively low paying job or spend more time with my new daughter; I was instantly able to make the right decision for me.

If you are working through these numbers with me, you might wonder, what if my income is highly variable? Like all businesses, you need to look back over past results and make projections based on what you know. Projections are only your best guess based on the information at hand, and they should be on the conservative side. If you usually bring in revenues around X, projecting revenues of 3X probably isn't prudent. Actual results may vary for a million different reasons, but having a plan for your business, your money, and your time off starts here.

In this example, you'll see that the business can survive - and still support you - for three months of leave and nine months of a reduced work schedule, all because some savings (unallocated profit) were in place.

Take a moment now to complete your own version of this worksheet. A blank copy is provided in appendix G.

Super Simple Pregnancy Profit & Loss Snapshot ©	Pre-pregnancy monthly figures	Pregnancy (months remaining)	Maternity leave period (X months, starting when?)	Post-baby ramp-up period (X months, starting when?)
Monthly Revenues				
(minus) Monthly Expenses- fixed				
(minus) Monthly Expenses- variable				
(equals) Monthly Gross Profit				
(minus) Required salary				
(equals) Monthly Unallocated Profit (savings) or Loss				
Reserves (amount in your business checking account)				

That's it. If you did this much financial planning, you are doing more than most small business owners ever do. If you have your expenses and revenues in a program like QuickBooks, completing the expense projections and the Super Simple Pregnancy Profit & Loss Snapshot© above will be easy. You now know if you can take time off, and how much time based on your current snapshot. If you don't like the answers, you'll need to change the inputs. In order to do that, continue reading below. You might also schedule some time with a mentor or CPA to get more financial advice.

Savings

If you have savings in your business, congratulations, your new baby is why you have been saving. If you don't have savings in your business, do you have some time to plan before your delivery? Look at the revenue side of the equation to see if you can increase it, and look at the expense side to see if you can reduce it, so that you can build up some savings.

You may already be saving money in your business, or this may be a completely new concept to you. Unfortunately, the decade of the 2000s has shown that too many people are personally unprepared to temporarily live off of their savings. In

2010, personal savings rates nationally were six percent, which means only six percent of paychecks went unspent according to the US Commerce Department.[45] This figure has been as low as one percent in the early 2000s, and we can extrapolate that into the business community. One of the most commonly cited reasons for business failure is undercapitalization, which is another way of saying there isn't enough savings to sustain daily and major financial needs. Businesses, just like people, need to save for a rainy day.

How do you set up a savings plan for your business? First, especially if your business is a sole proprietorship, partnership, or LLC, ensure that business and personal finances are separated. Establish a business account to be used exclusively for your businesses revenues and expenses. Second, even if your business is run on an only- or mostly-cash basis, ensure that all income is recorded in your accounts, and that all expenses are paid from your business account. This sounds simple and basic, and it is. In fact, for the first year that I was in business, I didn't even open a separate checking account, but I started using a dormant checking account for the business only. A business bank account today may not even cost you anything besides the cost of the checks, but it is an extremely helpful tool for you. The IRS really likes to see that you are maintaining separate business records, which is one more way to prove that your business is not a hobby.

The easiest way to figure out how much you can save is to simply deposit all of your income into your business account (whether your customers pay you by checks, cash, credit cards, or PayPal), and to pay all of your bills from this account. Then withdraw your salary on a regular basis from the business account. What is left will be unallocated profit, otherwise known as owner's equity, which is your savings from business operations. Unless your business is a corporation with external stakeholders, that is your money to spend as you see fit, even though it sits in your business account as unallocated profit until it is withdrawn.

What should you withdraw as your salary and when? Give yourself a regular pay day, but you aren't just an employee anymore. Like so many things in business, you wear multiple hats; you are the accounts receivable manager and the accounts payable manager. So when you pay yourself, make sure that you also get all the business deposits in, and then pay your business bills. This makes sense, when you think about it, since you want to make regular deposits to ensure you have funds to pay your business bills. Depending on your revenues, how close you are to your bank, and how often you need to withdraw funds, you may choose to do this weekly, twice a month, or monthly. If you haven't already been doing this, then start on a weekly basis, just as if you were getting a paycheck from an employer. If you are responsible for employee payroll, then enter accounts payable and accounts receivable as often as you complete payroll. This just means making deposits, paying bills, writing payroll checks, and paying yourself all at the same time.

The amount you can take out as salary should have already been determined in the section above. If you still aren't sure, or if you are concerned that there might not actually be any profits to draw from, start with a nominal amount, as little as $25 or $50 a week. Once you see your account balance stabilize, you'll be able to adjust your salary to accommodate both your account balance and living needs. Hopefully the amount you are paying yourself is fairly close to the answer to the question we asked earlier: How much do you personally need to get paid?

At this point, this should sound familiar. This is probably similar to how you run your household. Running your business isn't rocket science, and you don't need a business degree. Just remember that you are in business to make money, and that means making profits on the bottom line, not just revenue on the top line.

Many computer programs can help you complete the steps above. If you've been in business for more than five years, you are probably already utilizing a program such as QuickBooks, Quicken, or Microsoft Money. Your checkbook register or a computer spreadsheet can help you accomplish the same task at no cost. I don't recommend this, however, as these methods limit your ability to do analysis, limit your ability to handle an audit well, and can also limit your ability to account for certain types of transactions, such as receivables paid with cash and cash that you keep on hand.

Like everyone else, your small business is required to file and pay taxes. If you are running a very small business, you may enter your revenues and expenses yourself, without a bookkeeper. By doing the steps above, you'll organize and simplify your finances so that your meetings with a CPA are productive and painless. An accountant or CPA is an excellent resource. They can save you much more than you might spend on missed deductions or tax errors.

Why discuss these savings and financial housekeeping details here? Because you will enjoy your time with your new baby more if you have a good handle on your finances and if you are sure that the time you spend working is profitable. If you doubt either statement, you are likely to either bury your head in the sand and allow your financial condition to deteriorate without analyzing it, or you will hurry back to work to re-establish income, when it may not be profitable income.

Pregnancy, especially if this is your first baby, is the perfect time to figure out the systems to solve your business dilemmas. You'll never again have as much free time as you do right now.

Financing

Most businesses in the United States today are small businesses. In fact, over 89 percent of American businesses employ less than twenty people, while 60 percent have fewer than five employees.[46] There are all different types of businesses. However, one differentiator may be the debt-free business versus the business that requires heavy investments or financing. Typically businesses like franchises and manufacturers require an investment. This debt, or more accurately, servicing this debt and interest, becomes part of your expenses. Debt is a common but often crippling feature of modern life. Interest payments steal your profit and your ability to save for the future. Without debt and interest, your financial model can help you to make choices that are good for you, instead of making choices that are good for the banks and your creditors. If you'd prefer not to have debt, translate your skills developed in previous jobs or hobbies into businesses where your only up front investment is your computer and the home office desk or kitchen table that it sits on. Accounting, writing and editing, tutoring, professional sewing, personal training, dog grooming and many professions are examples of this.

You know what it takes to run your household, and you probably try to live within your means. The good news is that you can probably do the same for your business, using its own revenue to support it, without taking on additional debt. The key is to keep an eye on the revenue and, like you do at home, not spend more than your business generates.

Thousands of small businesses start and run without debt every day. The SBA states, "There are many business types, however, that do not require a hefty up front investment or can be started with grants and aid. Small businesses rely heavily upon owner investment and bank credit, averaging about $80,000 a year for young firms. Startups rely about equally on owners' cash injections into the business and bank credit;

young firms receive about three-quarters of their funds from banks via loans, credit cards, and lines of credit. *One-tenth of startups and about a third of young firms do not use capital injections.*"[47] (emphasis added) Because most small businesses are private, meaning they don't have to report their financials to anyone but the IRS, and because most small business finances are tied up with the personal finances of the owner, you don't read much about this. But if you do your homework, with the aid of a few spreadsheets and projections, you can figure out how to operate within your means.

If your business is already carrying debt, it is possible to restructure your business so that you can pay off that debt and remain debt-free in the future. It takes discipline and prioritizing, but since children change everything, they can change this, too.

Debt-free living is back in fashion. There's no better feeling than having enough financial security to be able to do what you love and live like you want to live, even in the middle of a recession.

Taxes

A dollar you do not pay in income taxes is a dollar that you earn. If your business is small, or even if it is teeny-tiny, pay attention to your tax situation and the tax laws, which change every year. You might not be an expert on the subject, but by learning a little, asking lots of questions, and having a very good CPA on your team, you can make sure that you are keeping as much of your earnings as possible.

Did I lose you yet? Most small business owners tune out when the subject of income taxes come up. But saying that your bookkeeper takes care of your taxes is about as silly as saying that your dentist takes care of your teeth. You may think that taxes are a dry and boring subject, but stuffing cash in your pockets is never boring.

If you have very little grasp on you tax situation, set up

the easy tried and true twelve-envelope system (or a twelve-pocket accordion folder) to store any and all receipts related to your business by month, and discuss all receipts with your CPA. Here's a brilliant thought: you don't actually have to file things into categories, especially when you might not have the foggiest ideas what those accounting categories might be. Use some kind of bookkeeping software for your business, like QuickBooks. Just separate your business from personal expenses, allow your bookkeeper to make the electronic entries, and you'll be able to slice and dice any reports you want from there.

What kinds of things can give you a tax break? It may be more than you think. Sure, all of your direct costs, like costs for your products, shipping, and extra phone line are deductible business expenses. However, so is auto mileage for your business activities, which can legally include side trips for household errands. Rather than taking mileage, it may be better for you to take a portion of your actual expenses for the car and its upkeep. Check with your tax advisor often. Sometimes there are improved benefits for certain types of vehicles, as was the case in 2010. Mileage rates change yearly or more. Selling your car can also yield positive tax results if you plan ahead and follow tax rules.

The costs of going into business, if that's the stage you are in, are also deductible. Not only the obvious, like buying new equipment, but even placing items in service that you already own can earn you some deductions. Sure, you've owned your desk for a hundred years, but the minute you turn it into a business asset, you can deduct its value. Also, any research, training, and marketing that you pay for before you actually start your business can be deducted, if you follow the IRS rules.

Business books, education, association dues, and professional fees such as those for your lawyer or CPA are also deductible. You can still muddle through your own Do It Yourself tax software if you want, but I don't recommend it. Learn enough about taxes to ask good questions so neither you nor your CPA leaves money on the table. The IRS has a pretty consumer-friendly information site at www.IRS. gov. In addition to finding tax forms, you can search on terms like "hobby" or "business deductions" and come up with some very readable tip sheets, bulletins, and reports.

Here's where it gets fun. You can deduct fifty percent of the cost of most meals and entertainment when it relates to business. So those lunches and dinners that you share with actual or potential business prospects now are deductible. When you are in business for yourself, when are you not talking about the state of your business, after all? It stinks that the deduction is only fifty percent, but it's better than nothing. If your business is really small, this might actually be an incentive to entertain more and make those social connections that will allow you to grow your business.

Just like entertainment, you can also turn travel into a business expense. Many, many successful people never take vacations (which are not deductible), but take many trips with and without their families that are entirely or partially deductible. Be very careful that you follow the rules here, and listen to your tax advisor. If you take a cross country trip to visit grandma each year anyway, why not make some or all of the trip deductible? If you travel for your job, there might be opportunities to have your family join you in some of the more happening spots for some R & R. Remember that babymoon that my husband I and took to Quebec before our first child arrived? If I had known then what I know now, I would have planned a day of work with a colleague in that area (I could track one down through my professional association) and could have made the whole trip tax deductible as a business trip. It all would have been perfectly legal. Deductions don't make things free, remember, but they make them tax-efficient, which means the real cost of a trip like that would be about twenty-five to thirty percent less than you actually paid for it.

Software and technology are also deductible business

expenses, so keep track and be sure to follow the depreciation rules. You may be able to take the full deduction in the year you made the purchase, under the Section 179 deduction from the IRS. Honestly, I start to black out when my CPA says the word depreciation, so I'd advise you to get professional help on this one.

Another favorite of mine is charitable contributions of both cash and goods. If, like me, you wish to support causes through your business, you can make donations of cash and goods for marketing purposes that are deductible. Remember that deductible expenses lower your taxable income. Unfortunately donations of services are not deductible, so you may offer a $100 deductible donation to one of your favorite charities in exchange for a mention in their newsletter (this is marketing), but you can not donate the equivalent of $100 of your services and take a deduction. Cash donations offered from your business account may be more tax efficient than if they were written from your personal household accounts, so check with your advisor.

These are just the top deductions that you might not know you could be taking as a business owner. Research these and others that you might be missing. This year, you'll need every bit of help you can get to finance the time off that you want to be taking.

The first time my CPA told me that my goal was to not have any taxable income, I was confused. The more I learned about deductions and tax planning, the more I understood that top line revenues and taxable income are only related, and they are not the same thing. You will be doing yourself, your family, and your business a favor to learn more about how this works.

Insurance

There are a few things to investigate regarding insurance when you own your own business and are having a baby. The first is business liability insurance. If your business carries liability insurance or specialized policies like errors and omissions insurance in the professional trades, call your carrier just to review your policy. By the way, this is a good thing to do every few years anyway. In addition to ensuring that you carry adequate coverage for your business, you may also want to ask whether there might be a portion of your policy that you could suspend or reduce while you are out caring for your newborn. The premium reduction might not be significant, or the risk to reducing coverage for a period of time might make you pause, but it is worth investigating. I chose to keep all of my policies in full force during the time I was on leave. Insurance is one of those fixed costs that we planned for earlier.

Another good question to ask is whether your policy includes any type of disability coverage that would apply for your maternity leave. It is unlikely that you would have this without realizing it. But by all means, ask the question and see if there is any benefit coming to you.

State and federal unemployment compensation will almost certainly not be available to you, as it is unlikely that you have paid into your state's unemployment compensation for yourself as a small business owner. Even if you have, you probably are not intending on closing your business, and will continue to be employed in your business while you are on leave. However, labor laws change all the time, so you check again with your state's labor board and with your insurer.

Health Insurance

It is beyond the scope of this book to cover all the intricacies of the health insurance policy that covers you. The Health Care Reform Act of 2010 will undoubtedly change health insurance in the coming years in ways we don't fully anticipate just yet. The simplest thing is to call each of your insurance providers, if you are covered by more than one policy, and find out what benefits will apply to you.

You'll want to know about things like in-network providers, co-pays, covered maximum charges, routine procedures (like ultrasounds) that might not be covered, alternative therapies like deliveries at non-hospital birthing facilities, pharmaceutical coverage, and supportive therapies like nutritional counseling and massage therapy. Check both your coverage and your spouse's coverage. Find out which coverage will pay first and second if applicable. Your health insurance policy exists to pay for covered medical expenses, but will not subsidize any of your lost income.

Disability Insurance

The one type of policy that may, indeed, provide you with some additional income is a disability policy, if it is in force before you get pregnant and does not contain a pregnancy exclusion. This topic is a double edged sword. We live in a time when we are enlightened enough to know that pregnancy is not a disability or illness, but a natural state. We have many more rights and protections as pregnant women, but we typically have few income replacement sources as women business owners. You would have to purchase disability insurance in advance of your medical condition (your pregnancy) for it to be of any benefit to you. Although it may be possible to purchase a disability policy while pregnant, your current pregnancy will be considered a pre-existing condition and will be excluded from benefits. If you already have a disability policy, especially one from an employer, you should look into what it covers. Some types of pre-existing conditions may worsen during pregnancy, or situations may arise that require your doctor to reduce or eliminate your work load prior to delivery. In most cases disability starts at labor and ends when you have recovered from delivery, which is only a few weeks. In order to be eligible for disability payments through your own small business policy, you often must document your earnings over a period of time to your insurance company, who then would insure a portion of your income in the case of disability.

The nice thing about disability payments is that they are often taxed differently than regular income, or not at all. The bad thing about disability insurance is that if you are running your business tax-efficiently and have low or no profits (not revenues), there will be nothing to insure.

A disability policy may provide short-term benefits, long-term benefits, or both. It may or may not provide maternity coverage. A disability policy is not the same as AD&D coverage, or accidental death & dismemberment. While it is common for an employee to have short-term disability coverage which replaces lost income during the postpartum period, policies are widely available at the group level and less common for individual business owners. The best thing to do is to contact your insurance carrier or a professional benefits consultant with experience in disability insurance, and find out what is provided under your policy, and do it before you get pregnant.

Multiple Income Streams

Chances are you started your business as a sole practitioner or as an owner/manager with a small staff. When you are healthy and childless, you can focus great amounts of energy on your business. Hard work during the start-up phase of business can be exhilarating.

But if, like me, you left your ten-hour a day job and find yourself working twelve-hours a day in your new business (seven days a week), something has to adjust to allow you to be the work-at-home mom that you dreamed about being.

The internet and today's technology allow us to be plugged in and always available. You get to figure out how to mesh technology and your business together to become the professional entrepreneur who also enjoys her time with her family, wherever that may be. With the remaining time that you have in your pregnancy, map out how you are going to use technology, and not become a slave to it. It is possible to move beyond the sole practitioner or owner/manager model to create income streams that continue even while you are at the beach, at the zoo, or even catching a well-earned nap.

- Bring on additional staff or consultants and send them out to do hands-on work that you previously did.
- Refer work out to other professionals, collecting referral income from those alliances.
- Develop information products like books, articles, DVDs, or streaming information that your customers buy directly from the internet.
- Create a subscription program delivering targeted content to your audience on a regular basis.
- Develop a product that you have manufactured and delivered through your website or traditional retail channels.
- Maintain investments, like renting vacation properties or partial ownership in another business, to provide additional income.

These income streams might increase your flexibility when it comes to planning your time with your newborn. If this sounds right for you, go back to your Super Simple Business Plan© and do the task planning and the financial planning to figure out how you can add this type of income to your activities.

Information Products

The new rich, as described in the book, *The 4-Hour Workweek* by Timothy Ferriss, is a phenomenon that comes out of the newest technology and information products. Information products are created once and sold to a large audience via automated tools. Do you have some special skill, system or story that people are willing to purchase through the internet?

The ultimate information product is a book. Not everyone wants to write a book, and writing a book will not necessarily make you rich, but you might be able to offer other types of information products to your website or sales portfolio that will produce income even if you are not personally meeting with a client. You sell things online like live teleconferences, podcasts, web seminars (also called webinars), online books or e-books, and other information tools.

If your baby hasn't yet arrived, plan, execute, and begin selling those information products in your business. Researching, creating, and marketing those tools will take time, but sleepless nights that you spend on them now can actually be productive. The sleepless nights you spend after the baby arrives are likely to be completely different and not conducive to revenue-generating activities. You can find out exactly how to create these information products by, you guessed it, searching on the internet. Because new technologies are literally popping up every day, the web will be the best place to research.

You can be successful with information products by reading as much as you can on the topic and by asking someone you know who is already successful. It continues to amaze me how much you can learn by just asking someone how they became successful. Chris Gardner, whose memoir was popularized by the 2006 movie *The Pursuit of Happyness*,[48] credits his rise to success with this simple principle of asking a successful person, "How do you do what you do?" I've used it over and over again myself. People who are successful in their chosen endeavor are almost always pleased to be asked about their experiences, and are generally happy to share with you, an appreciative listener. Valuable insight often costs just the price of a cup of coffee or a shared lunch.

Retirement

This is one topic you may not have seen coming in this chapter. Pregnancy is all about new beginnings, and retirement seems more about the end. Still, advance planning for retirement now can put your little one and your whole family on firmer foundations. If you or your spouse ever worked for a corporation, chances are you had access to a 401K retirement plan. They are great because the company you work for usually matches a percentage of the amount that you are socking away in pre-tax contributions for your own retirement. But once you are on your own, you don't have the luxury of someone else padding your retirement account. Not only that, but most women who own small (and teeny-tiny) businesses aren't getting the kind of financial advice that employees in larger companies may be getting.

Women are often at financial risk because they take years away from the workforce or start lifestyle businesses that offer great flexibility and quality of life, but sometimes at the expense of higher paychecks. Add in the risk of divorce or other family catastrophe, and our stability in retirement years can be put at great risk.

How great would if be if you could put yourself personally and your family on better long-term footing? Small businesses can set up a retirement plan that acts like a 401K. Both the SEP and the SIMPLE are retirement accounts that you can set up that are funded by your business. They can be a little tricky to administer, so have a CPA help set up and administer them. Like a corporate 401K, you make your retirement account contributions from your business income, not your personal income like you would with a ROTH or traditional IRA. By making contributions from your business income, you decrease your business income and therefore pay fewer taxes. The money is wrapped up in a retirement account that is restricted to age and other limits, but it is still your money and it is still growing for your retirement. There are limits to how much you can contribute, but by contributing the maximum allowed each year, you might essentially wipe out all or nearly all of your taxable profits from a very small business, reducing or eliminating income taxes. At a time in your life when you are spending for baby, take care to create an efficient retirement plan. Fund your retirement early because, although you might be able to borrow for household or college expenses, you can't borrow late in life to fund your retirement.

The New Baby

So far, we've been planning your business and personal finances in a nearly perfect vacuum. But you'll be adding a new cuddly little factor into your equation very soon. In fact, you'll probably start to spend on Junior before he even comes home from the hospital.

Baby expenses that might start to mount even before the little one arrives include additional medical expenses. If you have a medical plan, find a medical provider that works within your insurer's plan so that the maximum amount of your expenses can be covered. Insurance co-pays, which might only be $10 or $20, can add up week after week, especially if you need to be seen by specialists, who will each require their own co-pay.

New baby items will certainly start creeping into your spending. Hold off as long as you can, since you may really be surprised at the generosity of friends and near-strangers. A friend who lived in the city was showered with gifts from a complete stranger who she randomly met on the street one day. Seeing that my friend was pregnant, the stranger offered an entire car full of baby gear, toys, and clothes that her two-year-old had outgrown. Since all of it was in great condition, my friend saved hundreds, if not more, through the stranger's generosity. Fulfill your shopping desires by window-shopping and creating your baby registries, in stores or online. Let friends know that you have registered and where. Even if you can't really register for that one special boutique item not found at the store where you built your registry, you may find that gift cards and cash gifts for your new bundle will help you bankroll their purchases. When I heard about one family who spent over $2,000 on a crib, all I could think of was how crazy I'd be when the baby started using it as a giant teether, as both of my girls have done. I know you are going to stumble on that perfect homecoming outfit for Junior, but please listen to me. Conserve your cash!

Besides, babies are really simple. Despite all the marketing to convince you otherwise, they only require the basics. They need a car seat if you are driving them home, a place to sleep, diapers, nutrition, and basic clothing. Anything else is gravy, and can be borrowed or bought later if you don't receive it as a gift. Use these guidelines to keep your baby budget lean, especially when Junior is small, which will allow you to spend more time at home if that's what you want to do. If it helps with self-control, think of each additional baby item you purchase as one day earlier that you'll have to cut your maternity leave short.

While your nesting instinct is kicking in, you should also pay close attention to your business finances, whether or not you love the numbers. With these Super Simple Plans and the marketing tools in the next chapter, you'll have an easy way to generate and keep track of the money while running your business with plenty of time left over for cuddling your baby.

Critical Questions:

- What living and daily expenses does your business need to finance?

- What are your attitudes about money? Does your partner share them?

- Is your business already covering your business expenses, your salary requirements, and enough profit to allow for growth?

- Does your business have savings that would allow you to finance your desired maternity leave?

- Do you have any insurance benefits that you might be able to tap?

- What new income streams can you get up and running before your due date?

The Fourth Trimester

Ready for some more new math? Welcome to the fourth trimester, otherwise known as the first three months with your brand-new baby. Plan, research, and be prepared for change as much as you can. Your days in the fourth trimester will soon be upon you, and you'll learn on the job by being a mommy 24/7.

Having help in the first few hours, days, weeks, and months is such a gift. If possible, line up additional help for those first crucial days at home. If your spouse has time available through paternity leave or vacation from his work, consider staggering his time with another family member so that you don't have your mom, best girlfriend, and husband all staring at your brand-new baby at the same time. Scheduling assistance might take some tact and negotiating, but having only one capable person at a time to help you over two or three weeks is a much better situation. For us, that meant my husband had to go immediately back to work and take his vacation during week two of our new baby's time at home, while the grandparents got the first week with us, due to their work and travel schedules.

Hormones are a powerful thing. In childbirth class they mention the baby blues. If you find yourself reacting to commercials or TV story lines in a strange way, that's totally normal. After our daughter was born, we were asked to certify that we knew what shaken baby syndrome was and that we would protect against it, and just the request in itself almost set me over the edge. A friend cried uncontrollably after each birth, but was never sad. On the flip side, I know it sounds hard to imagine, but if you have a positive birth experience, you may return home in the first few days feeling like you can leap small buildings in a single bound. That may be true until sleep deprivation catches up with you and you decide that leaping small speed bumps is worthy of an Olympic medal. My point is that hormones are unpredictable, even in those of us who are even-tempered, plan-ahead types. Be sure that you have a support system (mom, girlfriend, understanding spouse, or supportive physician) that you can rely on when you need to say, "You know, I'm feeling more sad than I think I should be at this point." Remind yourself that this is just the first of many mommy trials that you'll go through during the coming years. Some will be small and some will be large, but you need to have a safe way to tell it like it is in your world, and get help if you need it, whether that help includes prescription drugs or an extra dollop of whipped cream on your mocha.

Since it has probably been a few years since you pulled your last college all-nighter, this next one might be a shock for you, but you'll be stunned at just how tired you'll be in the fourth trimester. Since I didn't sleep in the last few months of either pregnancy, I thought I'd be prepared for the sleepless post-baby nights. The odd thing is that when sleeplessness is self-induced, it has a different effect than when it is induced by an eight pound bundle jarring your nerves at 11, 2, 4, 5:30, and 6 a.m. This middle of the night interruption is almost certain but fleeting. I have yet to meet any real mother without a nanny who actually gets sleep. For at least a few months, and sometimes a few years, your offspring will make demands on your sleep. Plan for it, and like the warning labels say, try not to operate heavy machinery while sleep deprived. Plan your rest and your work accordingly. Nap as often as possible, even if you think naps are for sissies. Four months after my second baby arrived, I was still trying to steal a nap at least once a week, especially since sleeping late in the morning was no longer possible because of my toddler. Fourteen months after my second baby, I was still napping occasionally and not always admitting to it. The middle of the night is actually great bonding time with your baby. There probably isn't a lot going on in the world that requires your attention at 2 a.m., so stay offline, nix the TV, keep your lights dimmed, and try to figure out what the heck this tiny little human is trying to tell you. This is a great time, in fact, to learn what her biorhythms are, what voices she uses, whether or not she likes to snuggle. You will never get these hours back, and for that you may be grateful (kind of like junior high school), but try to embrace it and make the most of the bonding time.

If after the birth experience, the hormones, and the sleep deprivation you are still married to your spouse, just remember that he is also going to be walking-dead tired. Plenty of modern parenting books pontificate that to share that parenting load equally, both of you should share in the middle of the night duties. This is just nuts. Your lifestyle business gives you certain privileges, one of them being an unequal split of the parenting duties if you so choose. If your spouse has a more traditional corporate nine-to-five gig, especially if his job allows him valuable perks like healthcare and paid vacations, then let him operate at his best possible performance level by offering to take on the middle of the night work while you are on maternity leave from your business. That way he'll only be inconvenienced, and not incapacitated, those first few weeks. If he loves you and really is into shared parenting, there are plenty of things he can do to lighten your load that don't involve turning him into a sleepless zombie.

Plan, plan, plan, and then be flexible. How much time to take off from your business is something you've spent a lot of time discussing, planning, and anticipating. Now that time off is here. My advice is to be flexible. As a small business owner, you probably knew that you don't really get to take time completely off, didn't you?

You may try to be completely unplugged for a period of time, and then re-enter on your defined schedule. But then you decide that you'll just check email innocently enough, and suddenly you are back online for two or more hours a day. Or you may decide you want more or less time out of the action than you thought you would. Any answer is OK, as long as it is OK for you, your partner, and your child. Since you don't have an HR department you must answer to, or a set of federal guidelines that limit your options, you get to call the shots.

The second time around, my timeline looked like this:

At two weeks post-baby, I was still trying to close out the last few items from before my delivery. I had three clients with issues outstanding. Luckily, all of them knew my situation, and were willing to be patient. I sent new leads to a colleague, under an arrangement we crafted weeks before the birth. Offering business to a colleague and not actually having to turn clients away without a solution felt good, and I earned a small fee for handing over those leads.

At four weeks post-baby, I attended my monthly professional association meeting. It was great to be able to see my professional friends and brag about my girls a little bit. However, I knew I wasn't 100%, and would not have wanted to meet with clients.

At six weeks post-baby, I finally closed out the last of my client obligations. I was relieved, but at the same time, I was disgusted with myself that I'd had this hanging over me for the first six weeks with my baby. I would have preferred to have cleared all of these obligations earlier. I was also acutely aware that in a corporate environment, I probably would have been expected back at my desk full-time at that six-week mark. Thank God for small business.

At eight weeks post-baby, even though I had planned for a three-month leave period, I met with a client via phone after the girls' bedtime. My husband was willing to run interference if the new baby needed attention during my call. Between this and other small projects that I was getting done during naptimes, I was exhausting myself. Worse, I was actually losing sleep because of commitments that were running through my head. I finally had to admit that I was working too hard, and I re-evaluated where I was spending my time. I started making more appointments for playdates, coffee breaks, and naps.

At ten weeks, I had almost decided to extend my maternity leave by another two months. I was reconsidering my childcare needs for the spring, and trying to determine a reasonable work schedule through the next six months. I determined that one weekend day and one weeknight, with a maximum travel plus work time of four hours per appointment, was going to be reasonable for me in the short-term. This put a real strain on my ability to take new clients, serve clients that are at the edge of my service area, address demand from existing clients, and bring in enough income for my business needs. Everything was negotiable on a daily basis. I decided that while my girls were small, it was more important to be around than to be rich.

Emails and cell phones and internet, oh my! I did turn off my phone during labor and delivery, which was a good thing, because I actually received a business call during that time. Boundaries, which are really tough for some people, are important. There really are some times when you shouldn't have to worry about your phone ringing; labor and delivery is one of them. No, there isn't a need to put an explicit message on your phone about why you aren't answering; a simple, "I'm not available right now, please leave a message," will work just fine.

I called an out-of-town friend a few years ago, just to catch up. I felt like an intruder when he said that he couldn't talk long because he and his wife were in the hospital awaiting their latest baby. It really had been too long since we had talked. I excused myself from the call immediately. Communicate to your clients as much as you feel comfortable with, but don't feel an obligation to answer every call or be available every minute. This is a special time when technology may not make things better.

You may imagine yourself back at your keyboard on day two, but you may run into surgery, complications, or more sleepless nights than you imagine, and not be able to, or want to, stay in touch as much as usual. Take steps to stay connected in ways that really make sense:

- Develop a need-to-know list months ahead of time, and have this list queued up for the big announcement, by whatever messaging method you like best (email, phone, snail mail, Twitter, text, etc.).

- Draft your birth announcement ahead of time, leaving only the details that need to be filled in after the birth (weight, time, etc.).

- If you are going to be out of communication for a time that would inconvenience others, consider placing an auto-response message on your email or voice mail. ("Hello, this is Darla, and I'm planning on being out of the office until December first. You may leave a message, but I'll be responding infrequently until I return on December first.")

- Consider having your spouse handle pressing personal messages and having an employee handle pressing work items. This may mean offering passwords to certain users, and then changing those passwords once you resume full control.

- Plan ahead by making sure that bills are paid on time, automatically or maybe even ahead of schedule, that subscriptions and memberships are renewed, and that work commitments are wrapped up as much as possible.

What If You Can't Continue?

It is possible that you decide after the baby arrives that you can't or won't continue with your business operations. Like life, babies can bring surprises. This may come out of necessity, like a baby who requires more care than most. Or it may be a happy event, if you decide that you love the full-time mom gig more than your business. In any case, it is worth asking this question now. What happens if you decide not to continue the business? Financially speaking, what would happen?

Would it be possible to sell your business, your brand, or your customer list? Do you have any obligations to a franchisor or licensor? Do you have any debt or other obligations to settle? Is this a business that you would simply like to put on ice indefinitely, with the option to resurrect it in the future? Or would the process be as simple as closing your doors, notifying your favorite clients, and removing your website from cyberspace?

There is one condition where you might decide that closing your business is the best thing to do. After a financial review like what is proposed in this book, if you determine that your business is not profitable, and you can't figure out how to get it profitable, or if you decide that you don't want to do what would be required to make it profitable, then closing the business and pursuing other efforts is completely reasonable. I've said it before, but running an unprofitable business is like doing volunteer work for free and agreeing to take a pay cut. Give yourself a deadline to produce a positive profit and loss report, and be as creative as possible about generating income in ways that are consistent with your business goals. At the end of the day, not every business will be lucrative enough to sustain the owner's income goals. The SBA reports the survival rate for small businesses is half at five years and a third at ten years after startup.[49] If you are not able to meet your income requirements, take your creative energy and apply it to the creative parenting phase of your life or to other interesting business opportunities, taking your hard earned experience with you. There are plenty of business ideas out there yet to develop.

Take some time to consider your exit strategy before your due date. Like drafting a last will and testament, no one wants to need it tomorrow, but it does make the next stage less of a hassle. If possible, talk with your CPA, a mentor, or a business advisor like those from the SBA or SCORE for pointers and planning.

You will likely be able to continue, and even thrive, in your business after you begin your family. Think of this exercise as one more point in your business plan, which allows you to put more energy into growing your operations.

Case Study

Kate owns an appraisal business that works with insurance companies, museums, galleries, and individuals. Her daughter was two years old and her business was well established when she became pregnant for the second time. She was in great health during the pregnancy, but her second daughter was born with medical complications. Her daughter spent eight weeks in the hospital NICU before coming home to meet her big sister. During the time her new baby was in the hospital, Kate was able to juggle many of her previous commitments. As she put it, some of her deals took months and years to engineer. She didn't want her clients to know about her family's troubles because her business might take years to recover from lost contacts. The downturn in the economy allowed her husband, who works in the construction industry, to be home more than usual. Between her husband, her parents who lived nearby, and her flexible schedule, she kept her business on track. But life with a medically fragile child is unpredictable, and many plans were changed on a moment's notice to be able to care for her business and her family.

Re-Entry

It's already been stated, but bears repeating. Healthy businesses don't just happen; they are planned. Whenever you intend to pick up your business activities, and at whatever pace you want that to happen, plan ahead. A plan can always be modified if required, but structure that you lay out ahead of time will provide you with both a guide and the reassurance that you are still in control of some things.

Before you start your maternity leave, ensure that key clients, suppliers, business partners, and employees know what your plan is for re-entry. Lay out your expectations and preferences for communication during your leave time. For instance, you may prefer that you receive only emails or cell phone calls, to lower the chances of your house phone ringing and waking the baby. You may establish that you'll check email only once a day, at approximately the same time each day, just to stay on top of things. You may establish with your staff that you will physically check in on your office or store once a week, but that you expect it to be a social visit, and not a problem-solving mission.

Once you are able to assume your business activities again, be clear on your schedule with yourself first. I really struggled with this for the first year. Once I had reliable childcare in place, I limited client meetings to only the hours that either she or my husband were available, and devoted the rest of my time to being a mom during the day. This made a huge difference in my business because I was less stressed when I was away from my daughter, and I only accepted jobs that would work within my schedule. I stopped trying to overbook my calendar in the fear that I wouldn't have any appointments at all in my new compressed work week. I still work six or seven days a week, but only three of them are days where I commute to client sites.

Booking clients and re-establishing momentum on marketing projects can be one of the biggest challenges to re-entry. Starting up that marketing engine can be tough after you've been out of the swing of things for a while. If marketing isn't your strength, you might need more than a little encouragement to regain your momentum. First, let's talk about your marketing plan. Marketing is really just telling your business story in four dimensions: price, product, place, and promotion. These are traditionally called the Four P's. With the Super Simple Marketing Plan© found in appendix H, you can briefly describe the Four P's for each of your services or business lines. Use more than one Super

Simple Marketing Plan© if you have more than one business or major product line. Having your plan in writing allows you simultaneously to clear your head of all those to-dos and to find the inconsistencies in your planning you never previously noticed. It also allows you to share your plans with your mentor, spouse, or advisors if needed.

Your Company's Super Simple Marketing Plan©

Price	Promotion
List your charges and price structure for each of your products or services. This is what you charge the customer, not what it costs you to provide the service or product.	List the top twelve activities you are either doing or plan to do to promote your business. Some of them will be repeatable activities and some may not be. Assign one to each month of the year if established, or one each week if you are in a start-up phase.
Place	**Product**
List the physical geography and the target demographics of your ideal client base. List all the places or ways that you might be able to get your product or service to clients, or distribution channels, such as in-home service, web, big chains, your retail store, affiliate sales teams, and more.	List your major services or products. If you have associated services or products, focus on the major income earners.

A marketing diary can be a very helpful tool if your focus is generating or ramping up revenues, and especially if you think of yourself as someone who isn't a natural marketer. When I kept a marketing diary, I used a simple blank, lined notebook and dated each page. My goal was to document three revenue-generating activities, such as calling a new client to follow up on a proposal, booking a date for a speaking engagement, or placing an ad for publication, before I left my desk for the day. Simple, but effective. I completed three tasks, then I allowed myself to go and do other things, such as catching up on email or reading up on the latest industry news, or even touching base with an encouraging (but not necessarily revenue producing) colleague. If other distractions did crop up during my day, I was able to honestly beg off by saying, "I'm sorry, but I'm right in the middle of something. Can I get back to you?"

Take a moment now to create your own marketing diary using the Super Simple Marketing Diary© found in appendix I. You can create this out of a blank spiral notebook or spiral bound index cards. Fill in each page or card with today's date and three marketing activities. Marketing activities are things like calling a potential client, booking an appointment, making a call to book a speaking engagement, placing a print advertisement, attending a networking event, making a follow up call to a networking contact, or any other activity that does or could result in additional revenue. You may also make copies of the blank page and keep a 3-ring notebook if you prefer.

Super Simple Marketing Diary © example
Today's Date: 12/13/2010

3 Marketing Actions:
1. *Called Carol to schedule appointment*
2. *Called library to schedule a seminar*
3. *Emailed vendor regarding holiday gifts for marketing to current clients.*

Done.

After days and weeks of feeling like you are getting nothing done on maternity leave, just accomplishing three things in a day for your business will be a serious victory. Even better, staying focused on the right three things every day will improve your business consistently. Those three things are likely to be cumulative. With this one little trick, you are likely to have made sixty or more new contacts during your first month back to work, which might only take you a few minutes during your little one's nap time. It's unbelievable, but some business owners don't accomplish that much in a non-pregnant state.

How to Make Your Leave the Best Time of Your Life

Time with your infant is precious. Whether you always dreamed of having a business and a family, or whether one or both were more of a surprise, this experience is unique in your life. Yes, entrepreneurship and parenting have some things in common, among them, the fantastic opportunity to get things wrong an enormous amount of the time. They also have in common the chance to change you for the better and leave something bigger than yourself. This fourth trimester will be just the beginning of that.

Even if you think you can or should go back to work immediately, take the time off when you can. Things that can wait for later, should. Take the time now to be at home and fully present in your new role before you try to flawlessly blend the two, because flawlessness will be elusive.

Enjoy the baby. It goes so fast. At ten weeks postpartum, I was already mourning the first baby hair that fell out, the outgrown newborn outfits, and the little coos that soon turn into primitive words and gestures. That well worn statement- it goes so fast- is too true to be just a cliché. There is nothing in the most recent five years of my business that I couldn't have put off for a few months if needed, but that isn't true of a baby. Forget the fact that you are saddled with the thankless chore of changing diaper after diaper without much to show for it. Experts tell us that every time we make eye contact, every time we touch our child, every time we read her a story, we are helping to make neural connections that weren't there yesterday and might not be made in quite the same way by someone or something else. Thoughts and emotions can range everywhere from, "All I want to do is cuddle, bills be damned," to, "Why can't this baby be quiet five minutes so I can send off this one message?" It might help to test your activities against the five-year rule. This, very simply, is asking yourself whether this activity or thing that is giving you anxiety will make a difference in five years. If the answer is yes, then it deserves your attention. If the answer is no, then there may be something, or someone, else that deserves it more. Babies are the ultimate long-term investment, and the buy and hold strategy needs to be taken literally.

Take the time to do a baby book, as corny as it may sound. If you have no other way to gain perspective (and perspective may be very lacking in a sleep deprived state), then the baby book, or whatever way you decide to capture first memories, will help you ground yourself. I like the type of baby book that gives you space to record the important events of each month. A month seems to be about the right amount of time to record a paragraph of significant events. While I was able to keep up the schedule for baby number one, I was already in month three for baby number two before I made the time to sit and write that paragraph. If baby books aren't your thing, that's OK, too. Any box will do to collect and contain your memorabilia. Months or years from now, it will be fun to see what you collected when you could barely remember what your new baby's name was.

This fourth trimester is a tricky one, balancing new baby, body troubles, work stuff (or ignoring work stuff), and your spouse. But don't forget the woman behind the mommy. Get out there with other humans. Make playdates for your older children with parents you really want to hang with. Hire a sitter for the afternoon and get your nails done. Stay connected to networks that have loose attendance expectations. Find a mom's group that meets your needs. Make coffee dates with friends for when the kids are in bed and your husband is willing to cover for you. After your doctor clears you at about six weeks postpartum, find a physical activity you like and do it, whether that means hitting the gym, taking belly dancing, finding a dance DVD with great music, or hiking the trails. When you find time to be fit, you have so much more energy, which comes in handy with the kids and the demands of an entrepreneur's life. For heaven's sake, do something, because no one else is going to make sure you get time for you.

If you are taking time off from your always-on job of entrepreneur, won't you get bored? This might just be a great time to learn something new, but then again maybe not. Consider that even ten hours of sleep might be broken four or five times by your new baby, meaning that you still wake up tired and cranky. Always loved cooking but never had the time to hang out in the kitchen? Guess what…your newest fan might let you entertain her from a highchair (placed a safe distance from the stove, of course) in your kitchen. Learning something new on your flexible schedule could really save your sanity. It's not a good idea, on the other hand, to spend money for classes that you can't attend or projects you don't have time to complete. If you decide to take on a new project at work, such as readiness for a new product launch post-baby, give yourself plenty of time to research and complete it without putting pressure on yourself or your staff.

Don't Forget the Good Stuff

I once heard a wonderful speaker, Scott McKain, end a very motivating talk by underscoring that we are all so busy building businesses, families, and lives, it is easy to miss the good stuff.[50] While there was much to take away from his presentation, this message of "not missing the good stuff" was right on target for me. It helps to ask why we take on a project or spend time on an activity. As an entrepreneur, you aren't pressured by some corporate manager's demands on your time. You get to design your day so it works for your old and new family members. From the frivolous to the serious, you get to call the shots. Under the heading of frivolous, I try never to make a commitment to be somewhere before 10 a.m., whether it is personal or for business. With two small kids in tow, and not being a morning person, my week just seems to roll better if I don't have to scramble in the early hours. Maybe that's not so frivolous, given that it means less yelling and stress in my home. I do have to make sacrifices because of my little rule, like avoiding breakfast networking meetings and a few clients who only want to work together in the mornings. But the why of my calendar always points me back to making a decision to run a business and care for my children. I want to have a relationship with my children, and that relationship building works better when I'm awake and not trying to wrangle everyone out the door.

Ten years ago, I never would have imagined myself doing certain things, like taking a morning walk in the park on a weekday, or joining a daytime Bible study program for an entire year. But today when I think about my reasons, I am able to make better decisions about how to spend my time.

When my first daughter was born, it seemed she always had the hiccups, but they were in miniature and very delicate, so we called them mouse hiccups. It was only a matter of months before she grew out of those teeny hiccups, which gave way to silly giggles, and then to toddler squeals. That silly sound that we make by blowing our lips on our child's tummy, also known as raspberries, is only welcome by our child for so long. There is a long list of these things that are here for weeks, months at best, before your adorable baby, then a toddler, then a child, won't tolerate them any longer. There are only so many trips down the park slide. There are only so many bedtime prayers. If you are paying attention to your baby as she is growing, like you have paid close attention to your business as you have been building it, you will get to experience the joys of mouse hiccups and raspberries and store them away before they are gone for good.

Plan your business. Be profitable. Enjoy your family. Chart your own course. Don't miss the good stuff.

Critical Questions:

- Why are you in business?
- What kinds of things pass the five year test? What kinds of things don't?
- What is your backup plan if you can't continue the business? Are there any assets that you might consider selling? How would you make the decision to temporarily suspend or end operations, if necessary?
- How will you arrange for personal help after the birth?
- What is your partner's expectation? Will he take some kind of leave as well? Does he have a flexible work arrangement that would allow each of you to take a chunk of time to spend with the new baby? Can he take a day off each week for a number of weeks to allow you to ramp up your routine?
- How difficult was it to have this baby? Did you require medical intervention to get pregnant? If so, will you emotionally be ready to leave your million dollar baby to someone else's care.
- How difficult do you anticipate your delivery to be? If you've had a challenging pregnancy, filled with medical

intervention, you might be headed for the same treatment in the delivery room. This in itself may make it difficult to pick up your work duties sooner.

- What is your plan for re-entering your work routine post-leave?

- What kinds of things will you do to re-ignite your marketing efforts?

- How will you make your leave a special time to be remembered?

Appendixes:

A. Super Simple Strategic Business Plan©

B. Birth Plan Example

C. Super Simple Weekly To-Do List© Example and Blank Form

D. Super Simple Staffing Support Plan ©

E. Board of Advisors Update

F. Maternity Leave Expenses Projection Tool

G. Super Simple Pregnancy Profit & Loss Snapshot©

H. Super Simple Marketing Plan©

I. Super Simple Marketing Diary©

Please visit
www.PregnantEntrepreneur.com
for downloadable forms from the appendix and
current articles on pregnant entrepreneurship.

Appendix A

Your Company's
Super Simple Strategic Business Plan©
(for Year_____)

Revenue	Team
Annual revenue target: _____ Annual salary target: _____ Retirement funding target: _____ Taxable income target: _____	(List all the members of your current team below. Also list separately the functions that you need to fill.)
Time	**Priorities**
Target work schedule: _____ Number of days per week: _____ Number of hours per week: _____ Maximum commute distance: _____ Training and education targets: _____	(List no more than 5 priorities to accomplish or nurture this year.)
Things I Need to Change	**Additional Revenue Streams**
(List items that you would like to make significant changes to in this current year.)	(List any possible revenue streams that you might explore, such as online sales, new vertical markets, or extensions of current business lines.)

Appendix B

Birth Plan Example for Littleone Lastname
We respectfully request the following:

The Birth Center Admission
(Hospital Admission if warranted)

- The patience and understanding to support our wish for the most natural birth possible.

- Artificial initiation of labor only if labor is unusually delayed and medically urgent.

- To remain at home as long as possible before going to TBC.

- To return home if < 4 cm opened and if there are no situations warranting admission.

- To be assigned caregivers who are partial to natural birthing.

- To self-hydrate and decline routine IV prep upon admission. Port OK if needed.

- Nutritional snacking allowed.

- Freedom to walk and move or not walk or move during labor.

- To change positions and assume labor positions of choice.

- To be free of blood pressure cuff and fetal monitor between readings.

- Min. number of vaginal exams- upon Mom's request- to avoid early membranes rupture.

- That labor is allowed to take its natural course without references to "augmenting labor".

- Natural means of inducement; min. doses of artificial induction only if medically urgent.

- To use natural oxytocin stimulation — nipple or clitoral stimulation- in the event of a slow or resting labor, and to be accorded the privacy to do so.

- To be fully apprised and consulted before the introduction of any medical procedure- augmentation, amniotomoy, membrane stripping, etc.

- To be referred to hospital only if medically necessary.

During Birthing

- Caregivers to allow Mom to initiate any discussion of pain management.

- HypnoBirthing approach with music and lighting; Dad directed coaching.

- Natural expulsive pulsations of the body be allowed to facilitate the gentle descent of the baby, with mother-directed Birth Breathing to crowning. Dad will offer prompts. No coaching needed by staff.

- To assume a birthing position of choice that will least likely require an episiotomy.

- Use of warm-oil compresses to avoid episiotomy. No perinatal massage to perineum.

- Episiotomy only if necessary and only after discussion and with topical anesthetic.

After Birthing

- Immediate skin-to-skin contact, with baby on Mom's lower chest, a blanket over both.

- Dad be allowed to cut cord after it stops pulsating.

- Dad to remain with mom in the operating / recovery room in the event of a c-section.

- Dad to hold baby after c-section birth and bring baby to mom for viewing & eye contact.

- Baby to remain with mom and dad for at least ½ hour following birth.

- Breastfeeding several times during the first few hours of baby's life.

- BREASTFEEDING ONLY. No bottles, formula, pacifier or artificial nipples.

We thank you in advance for your support and kind attention to our choices as we celebrate a beautiful birth and new life.

8-1-09

Appendix C

Example: Super Simple Weekly To-Do List©

Week starting : 12/13/10

20%
Send library speaker's agreement
Choose publisher
Have web developer implement site backups
Return software
80%
Call Carol to schedule 610-xxx-xxxx
Call Andy to renew contract 610-xxx-xxxx
Email printer with measurements
Order blinds for Jen
Do marketing plan for classes
Call CPA for end of year advice 610-xxx-xxxx
Complete healthcare claim
Post radio interview on website
Plan January program content
Schedule furnace maintenance
Schedule salon appointment
Confirm class registration for my daughter

Appendix C

Your Company's Super Simple Weekly To-Do List©

Week starting :

20%
80%

Appendix D

Your Company's
Super Simple Staffing Support Plan©

Function	Contact
Bookkeeping	
Board of Advisors	
Branded promotional items	
Certified professional accounting	
Childcare	
Childcare backup	
Contractors	
Employees and managers	
Graphic design	
Human resources and benefits	
Insurance	
Legal	
Marketing	
Photography	
Printing	
Service providers (e.g. painter, electrician)	
Suppliers, product vendors	

Appendix D

Technical/computer support	
Videography	
Virtual assistance	
Web design	

Appendix E

Board of Advisors Update
(Monthly or Quarterly)

RE: Update to Board of Advisors Members

Date:

- Top 3 goals & accomplishments in the latest period

- Most pressing challenge

- Top 3 goals in the upcoming period

- Assistance requested from Board members

Next meeting scheduled _____ via in person/ teleconference.

Appendix F

Your Company's
Maternity Leave Expenses Projection Tool
Period Covering Projected Maternity Leave: months/year

Date	Payment Type	Vendor Name	Memo/Description	Amount

Total Expenses (add
all lines above)

Salary- Owners Equity
@ $ / mo   +
Best Case Expenses for
Total Leave Period

Appendix G

Super Simple Pregnancy
Profit and Loss Snapshot©
for Maternity Leave

Super Simple Pregnancy Profit & Loss Snapshot ©	Pre-pregnancy monthly figures	Pregnancy (months remaining)	Maternity leave period (X months, starting when?)	Post-baby ramp-up period (X months, starting when?)
Monthly Revenues				
(minus) Monthly Expenses fixed				
(minus) Monthly Expenses variable				
(equals) Monthly Gross Profit				
(minus) Required salary				
(equals) Monthly Unallocated Profit (savings) or Loss				
Reserves (amount in your business checking account)				

Appendix H

Your Company's
Super Simple Marketing Plan©

Price	Promotion
List your charges and price structure for each of your products or services. This is what you charge the customer, not what it costs you to provide the service or product.	List the top twelve activities you are either doing or plan to do to promote your business. Some of them will be repeatable activities and some may not be. Assign one to each month of the year if established, or one each week if you are in a start-up phase.
Place	**Product**
List the physical geography and the target demographics of your ideal client base. List all the places or ways that you might be able to get your product or service to clients, or distribution channels, such as in-home service, web, big chains, your retail store, affiliate sales teams, and more.	List your major services or products. If you have associated services or products, focus on the major income earners.

Your Company's
Super Simple Marketing Diary ©

(You can create this out of a blank spiral notebook or spiral bound set of index cards. Fill in each page or card with this information. Marketing actions are things like calling a potential client, booking an appointment, making a call to book a speaking engagement, placing a print advertisement, attending a networking event, making a follow up call to a networking contact, or any other activity that does or could result in additional revenue.)

Today's Date:
3 Marketing Actions:
1.
2.
3.

Notes

[1] Centers for Disease Control and Prevention, National Center for Health Statistics, VitalStats page, February 4, 2010, http://www.cdc.gov/nchs/vital-stats.htm.

[2] Marcella Bequillard, "For Women Who Have Delayed Child Birth, Does Hope Hatch in Egg Freezing?" *MedicalNewsToday.com*, February 10, 2005, http://www.medicalnewstoday.com/articles/19853.php.

[3] CDC/National Center for Health Statistics, "American Women Are Waiting to Begin Families Average Age at First Birth up More Than 3 Years From 1970 to 2000," December 11, 2002, http://www.cdc.gov/nchs/pressroom/02news/ameriwomen.htm.

[4] Timothy Ferris, *The 4-Hour Workweek* (New York: Crown Publishing Group, 2007).

[5] Darcie Sanders and Martha M. Bullen, *Staying Home* (Boston: Little, Brown, 1992), 11.

[6] Ibid., p. 57.

[7] Malcolm Gladwell, *Outliers: The Story of Success* (Boston: Little, Brown, 2008).

[8] Lance Winslow, "Industry Jargon and Definitions Conflict with Common Language, " *Ezinearticles.com*, September 11, 2005, http://ezinearticles.com/?Industry-Jargon-and-Definitions-Conflict-with-Common-Language&id=70505.

[9] Denise and Alan Fields, *Baby Bargains: Secrets to Saving 20% to 50% on Baby Furniture, Equipment, Clothes, Toys, Maternity Wear and Much, Much More!* (Boulder, CO: Windsor Peak Press, 2006).

[10] Ari Brown, M.D. and Denise Fields, *Baby 411: Clear Answers & Smart Advice for Your Baby's First Year* (Boulder, CO: Windsor Peak Press, 2006).

[11] Katherine Ellison, *The Mommy Brain* (New York: Basic Books, 2005), 24.

[12] Tiffany Forte, "Expecting Respect," *Working Mother Magazine*, January 2010.

[13] Michael Port, *Book Yourself Solid* (Hoboken: John Wiley & Sons, 2006).

[14] Howard Taylor, "Time Management in the Age of Speed," National Association of Professional Organizers Annual Conference, Orlando, FL, May 1, 2009, Session 2-2.

[15] Marie F. Mongan, *HypnoBirthing: The Mongan Method* (Deerfield Beach: Health Communications, 2005), 36-37.

[16] Jeanette Curtis, "Depression: Managing postpartum depression," *WebMD.com,* June 24, 2008, http://www.webmd.com/depression/postpartum-depression/managing-postpartum-depression.

[17] Kristin Rothwell, "Survey Finds Increasing Number Prefer Personal Time Over Money, Hospitals Take Notice." Referencing *Salary.com* survey, *TravelNursing.com*, February 10, 2005, http://www.travelnursing.com/news/Survey-Finds-Increasing-Number-Prefer-Personal-Time-Over-Money-Hospitals-Take-Notice_31254.aspx .

[18] Craig H. Kinsley and R. Adam Franssen, "The Pregnant Brain as a Revving Race Car," *Scientific American*. January 19, 2010, http://www.scientificamerican.com/article.cfm?id=pregnant-brain-as-racecar.

[19] Katherine Ellison, *The Mommy Brain* (New York: Basic Books, 2005), 15.

[20] Ibid., p. 16.

[21] Maria T. Bailey, an author and owner of BSM Media, quoted in Jenny Staletovich, "Local mothers are the inventors of necessities," Miami Herald, November 12, 2007, http://www.inventionstatistics.com/Independent_Inventor_Statistics.html .

[22] Angela Shupe, "Mom's Invention Cleans the Grime Out of Sippy Cup Straws," Business Opportunities Weblog Network, March 25, 2010, http://www.business-opportunities.biz/2010/03/25/moms-invention-cleans-the-grime-out-of-sippy-cup-straws .

[23] Howard Taylor, "Time Management in the Age of Speed," National Association of Professional Organizers Annual Conference, Orlando, FL, May 1, 2009, Session 2-2.

[24] Michael Pollan, *Food Rules: An Eater's Manual* (New York: Penguin, 2009).

[25] Heidi Murkoff, Arlene Eisenberg, and Sandee Hathaway, B.S.N., *What to Expect When You are Expecting* (New York: Workman Publishing, 2002), 88-97.

[26] Heidi Murkoff and Sharon Mazel, *Eating Well When You're Expecting* (New York: Workman Publishing, 1986).

27 "Shoppers Guide to Pesticides," Environmental Working Group, 2010, accessed June 5, 2010, http://www.foodnews.org/sneak/EWG-shoppers-guide.pdf.

28 Richard E. Nisbett, *Intelligence and How to Get It: Why Schools and Cultures Count* (New York: W. W. Norton, 2010), 31.

29 Ibid., 184.

30 Ibid., 87-88.

31 Ibid., 90.

32 Katherine E. Wynne-Edwards, "Why do some men experience pregnancy symptoms such as vomiting and nausea when their wives are pregnant?" *Scientific American*, June 28, 2004, http://www.scientificamerican.com/article.cfm?id=why-do-some-men-experienc.

33 "Weight Gain During Pregnancy: Reexamining the Guidelines," National Academy of Sciences, May 28, 2009, http://www.iom.edu/Reports/2009/Weight-Gain-During-Pregnancy-Reexamining-the-Guidelines.aspx.

34 Nina Carbone, "Bra-Vo!," *The Bump*, 2009/2010, pp. 44-45.

35 Image of the Cantata home office armoire is courtesy of Riverside Furniture Corporation, www.Riverside-Furniture.com.

36 Denise Mann, "Pregnancy Brain: Myth or Reality? New research casts doubt, but most new moms beg to differ." WebMD, March 25, 2010, http://www.webmd.com/baby/features/memory_lapse_it_may_be_pregnancy_brain.

37 David Allen, *Getting Things Done* (New York: Penguin, 2002).

38 Atul Guwande, *The Checklist Manifesto: How to Get Things Right* (New York: Metropolitan Books, 2011).

39 Sarah Burns, "Fun Ways to Tell Your Husband You Are Pregnant," *American Baby*, May 2005, http://www.parents.com/pregnancy/my-life/preparing-for-baby/fun-ways-to-tell-your-husband-you-are-pregnant/.

40 BabyCenter Member ali0118, "What's the best way to tell my partner we're pregnant?" *BabyCenter.com*, January 7, 2004, http://www.babycenter.com/400_whats-the-best-way-to-tell-my-partner-were-pregnant_500479_1.bc.

41 A BabyCenter Member (unknown). "What's the best way to tell my partner we're pregnant?" *BabyCenter.com*. March 8, 2007, http://www.babycenter.com/400_whats-the-best-way-to-tell-my-partner-were-pregnant_500479_1.bc.

42 Tish Rabe and Dr. Seuss, *Oh, Baby, the Places You'll Go!: A Book to Be Read in Utero* (New York: Random House, 1997).

43 "Employee vs. Independent Contractor- Seven Tips for Business Owners, IRS Summertime Tax Tip 2010-20," *Internal Revenue Service*, August 10, 2010, http://www.irs.gov/newsroom/article/0,,id=173423,00.html.

44 Ramsey, Dave, *Financial Peace Revisited* (New York: Viking, 2003).

45 Ylan Q. Mui, "U.S. savings rate at highest level in a year, data show," *Washington Post*, August 4, 2010, http://www.washingtonpost.com/wp-dyn/content/article/2010/08/03/AR2010080305317.html.

46 "Statistics about Business Size (including Small Business) from the U.S. Census Bureau," *US Census Bureau* citing the 2002 Economic Census and Statistics of US Businesses , accessed February 21, 2011, http://www.census.gov/epcd/www/smallbus.html.

47 Alicia Robb, E.J. Reedy, Janice Ballou, David DesRoches, Frank Potter, Zhanyun Zhao, "An Overview of the Kauffman Firm Survey: Results from the 2004–2008 Data," Kauffman Foundation, May 2010, Quoted from US Small Business Administration. accessed June 5, 2010, http://web.sba.gov/faqs/faqIndexAll.cfm?areaid=24.

48 Chris Gardner and Quincy Troupe, *The Pursuit of Happyness* (New York: Harper Paperbacks, 2006).

49 "FAQs:Advocacy, Small Business Statistics and Research," referencing the US Dept. of Commerce, Census Bureau; Administrative Office of the US Courts; US Dept. of Labor, Business Employment Dynamics (BED). Estimates based on Census data and BED trends. Quoted from Quoted from US Small Business Administration website, accessed June 5, 2010, http://web.sba.gov/faqs/faqIndexAll.cfm?areaid=24.

50 Scott McKain, "What Clients Really Want," National Association of Professional Organizers Annual Conference, Orlando, FL, April 30, 2009, Opening Keynote Address.

CPSIA information can be obtained at www.ICGtesting.com
227650LV00002B/78/P